ALAN TITCHMARSH'S

FAVOURITE GARDENS

JARROLD
PUBLISHING

ACKNOWLEDGEMENTS

To all the gardeners and garden owners who have answered my questions during the writing of this book I am extremely grateful. Their hospitality and sustenance often threatened to get in the way of the visit! Thanks also to my editors, Paula Granados and Donald Greig, whose patience has been tested to the extreme. I can grow roses to flower in the fourth week in June but I have greater difficulty in delivering manuscript.
The photographers, Dennis Avon, John Brooks, Neil Jinkerson, Charles Nicholas, Andrew Perkins, Eric West and Jim Henderson have done a wonderful job in illustrating my favourite bits of my favourite gardens and have often leapt off at short notice praying that the weather would not let them down. I don't think it did.
And an especial thank you to one person in particular for her encouragement and her company. This book is for her.

ALAN TITCHMARSH'S FAVOURITE GARDENS

Designed and produced by
Jarrold Publishing
Whitefriars
Norwich NR3 1TR

Author: Alan Titchmarsh
Editors: Paula Granados, Donald Greig
Designers: Brian Skinner, Richard Snowball
Photographers: Dennis Avon, John Brooks, Neil Jinkerson, Charles Nicholas,
Andrew Perkins, Alan Titchmarsh, Eric West, Jim Henderson AMPA (Crathes Garden)

Text copyright © 1995 Alan Titchmarsh
Photographs © 1995 Jarrold Publishing except for Crathes Garden detailed above

ISBN 0-7117-0812-6

Printed in Great Britain 1/95

CONTENTS

INTRODUCTION

IT REALLY IS an impossible task. If you thought choosing eight records to take with you to a desert island was difficult, then you should try choosing your favourite gardens. 'Could the book be called "Some Favourite Gardens?"' I enquired.

'Afraid not', they replied; 'it sounds like a cop out.' And so, with furrowed brows and much rifling through garden guidebooks, I chose thirty-one of my all-time favourites and fussed for weeks about leaving others out.

For a start, I tried to ensure an even coverage of mainland Britain so that at least a handful of the gardens would be within reach of the reader wherever he or she lived. I've worked out that if you live in Kilmarnock you will have farthest to travel.

The National Gardens Scheme and The National Trust have, over the last fifty years, turned garden visiting into a national pastime. They have made more and more people aware of the pleasures of garden visiting. There are plants to be spotted and bought for your own garden, views to be admired and no responsibilities for the upkeep of beds and borders to be worried about. As Kenneth Grahame put it in *The Wind In The Willows*: 'the best part of a holiday is perhaps not so much to be resting yourself, as to see other fellows busy working.'

But it's not just the results of hard labour that appeal to me in my favourite gardens; it is the pouring in of personality. Oh, I can say 'gosh' or 'goodness me' at a bed or border that is bright and well tended, but the pleasure is shallow, not lasting. Gardens should offer more than neatness; they are individuals, often on account of the individuality of their creators, and I like to feel the influence of the garden maker as much as the maintenance team who have followed on. Even if it is now administered by The National Trust or some other large body, provided a garden is tended by gardeners who love it and who have a feel for its spirit, then it shows.

Some of my favourite gardens – such as Blenheim and Chatsworth – are large and stately, while others – 1 Lister Road and Sticky Wicket, for instance – are very small, but all of them are capable of giving me a lift on account of the fact that they click. Some gardens don't and it's not always easy to say why.

I can lose myself in a garden, and I don't just mean geographically. To look into a magnolia bloom or suddenly to come across a view of the surrounding countryside perfectly framed by a garden gate or an archway can take my breath away. Call me an old romantic if you want, but I like being moved by gardens.

What I've tried to do in this book is convey something of the atmosphere of each garden and how it made me feel. That may mean describing part of the journey I took to get there, or the people I encountered on my visit – they all contribute to my attitude to the place. The weather, too, can influence your opinion. I couldn't stand the Isle of Wight for years on account of the fact that it rained the first time I went there. I've been there since in sunshine and it's not unpleasant.

I feel rather guilty in confessing that the sun shone when I visited almost every one of these gardens. It gave me the problem of finding different ways of describing blue sky and emerald lawns, and views over the valleys and hills beyond. So if it rains or is foggy when you visit, then I'm sorry.

Are my descriptions all hearty and enthusiastic? Yes, mainly, because I think what's the point of choosing favourite gardens if all you want to do is nitpick. But now and again I've remarked on parts of a garden that I don't much like – a misplaced plant sales area or a nasty bed or border, and there is one garden here which I find fascinating on account of its history but which, in terms of its appearance, I could cheerfully leave within half an hour of my arrival. But that one is an exception and I'll let you decide which one it is.

Keen plantsmen may find that the book has too few Latin names. That's intentional; it's a book about gardens, not plants, and I want you to be won over by atmosphere and effect, not by botany. That said, I've not been afraid to let my enthusiasm run away with me when a particular plant or group of plants has left me bubbling with pleasure.

During the months it has taken to write this book I have had a wonderful time going back to my favourite gardens and confirming their place in my affections. I can remember every one of the thirty-one days with crystal clarity, so that if I pick the name of a garden from these pages I can take myself around it instantly once more. That's not a bad thing to be able to do.

My favourites may change over the years. Gardens, like people, do not stand still, but right now the thirty-one gardens you are about to discover are among the best in Britain. We may not produce the best tennis players, or the best cricketers in the world, but we do produce the best gardeners – and the best gardens. As the film-maker Derek Jarman said: 'Paradise haunts gardens, and some gardens are paradises.' That much is true, I hope, of the ones that I've picked.

SISSINGHURST CASTLE GARDEN

Kent

UNTIL 1969 I had never heard of Sissinghurst. Then I came, as a student, to Kew Gardens and lodged with Mr and Mrs Bell at Number 1 Willow Cottages just off Kew Green. My reading matter was Agatha Christie and Herbert van Thal. The music I liked was bound up with the musical theatre – everything from Rodgers and Hammerstein to Robert Stolz, Sigmund Romberg and Franz Lehar.

Mrs Bell raised an eyebrow. She enquired whether I would like to accompany her to the Queen Elizabeth Hall and St John's, Smith Square, to hear the London Sinfonietta and Chilean pianist Claudio Arrau. Perhaps I might enjoy the music of Benjamin Britten? She suggested, with only the gentlest of insistence, that I might enjoy The Wallace Collection and the Tate Gallery. She painted the door of her broom cupboard with voluptuous naked women holding bunches of grapes, bought me a copy of

OPPOSITE *The Rose Garden at Sissinghurst is stuffed with old-fashioned shrub roses that are richly underplanted. On the walls grow a fig and a climbing hydrangea.*

Under Milk Wood for my birthday, and talked about something called the Bloomsbury Group.

On her shelves were volumes about Viginia Woolf and her namesakes, the Bells. My Mrs Bell grew shrub roses like 'Vanity', 'Nevada' and 'Caroline Testout',

The view across the Herb Garden to the Elizabethan tower where Vita Sackville-West did much of her writing.

(instead of the hybrid teas I had hitherto thought of as the only proper roses) and there was talk of someone by the name of Vita Sackville-West and a garden in Kent called Sissinghurst that she had made with her husband Harold Nicolson.

My curiosity awakened, I bought the three volumes of Harold Nicolson's diaries. I read other books about Vita and her lover, Violet Trefusis, and found my whirling mind transported into a world of Bohemian passions and noble decadence, with talk of thick Turkish coffee and Arabian bazaars, travels in Tuscany and Samarkand.

I asked people who had been to Sissinghurst what it was like. Stories abounded of the lady who wore jodhpurs and high lace-up boots, who carried a hoe in one hand and a cigarette holder in the other, and who went about her garden with a German shepherd dog in tow, referring to her garden visitors as 'The Shillingses' – the price of the entrance fee. But that was a few years ago now. Vita Sackville-West had died in 1962, and Harold Nicolson six years later.

It was four years before I ventured there. I have the guidebook still, with the

The wall of the Moat Walk is overhung with climbers and opposite this is a bank of azaleas.

The Yew Rondel in the Rose Garden as seen from the tower. Beyond it is Harold Nicolson's Lime Walk – 'My Life's Work'.

date written on the spine: 15th June 1973. I can remember that day with crystal clarity. It was mid-afternoon. The garden was still – a warm June day in the Kentish Weald – the atmosphere electric. I walked through the building that contains the entrance arch and across to the Elizabethan tower. I climbed the stairs, quite alone, and looked through the wrought iron gate into Vita Sackville-West's study. There, on her desk, were the things I remembered from the photographs I had seen – a portrait of the Brontë sisters, a blotter, a Boots Diary and photographs of Virginia Woolf and Harold Nicolson.

I climbed to the top of the tower and gazed out over the countryside. Everything was warm and silent except for a blackbird singing in a far-off aspen. Below me, the garden was laid out in the pattern that I almost seemed to know by heart –

the Yew Rondel, the White Garden, the Nuttery, the Moat, and the strangely named Delos. I climbed down the tower and walked out into the garden and there, among the overpowering perfume of the shrub roses, my memories drown.

Now, more than twenty years later, the garden has become something of a shrine. It was given to The National Trust in 1967 and, until 1990, the two head gardeners, Pam Schwerdt and Sybille Kreuzberger (who had worked with Vita Sackville-West since 1959), remained in charge. Now it is down to Sarah Cook and her team of seven to keep the garden moving, not stagnant.

Yes, the features Vita and Harold created are still there, but to imagine that they are preserved artlessly is unfair. The box and yew hedges are immaculately trimmed, it is difficult to find a weed, and the colour scheming is carefully controlled (unlike Great Dixter, half an hour away, which is a wondrously extravagant mix); but to compare the two gardens is a

fruitless exercise. They can both thrill and delight in completely different ways.

Passing through the central archway between the Library and the Main House you enter a secluded world. When Vita Sackville-West first came here on a rainy day in 1930 the place was derelict, but the long, low house, dating from 1490, and the tower of the mid-sixteenth century so captivated her that she bought the property and the surrounding 400 acres within three weeks.

Over the next thirty years, Harold Nicolson designed the series of outdoor rooms and Vita was responsible for the planting. Their influences were Gertrude Jekyll, William Robinson and Major Lawrence Johnston at Hidcote Manor.

The White Garden is the most famous part of Sissinghurst. It was made immediately after the war and consists of a series of box-kerbed beds filled with all manner of white flowers and grey foliage. At its centre is an enormous umbrella of white-flowered *Rosa longicuspis* which once ran through a quartet of almond trees and which is now supported on an iron frame-work that turns it, in summer, into a vast floral parasol.

The Priest's House is adjacent to the white garden – one of the few buildings that could be restored when the Nicolsons arrived. Its roof is of dark brown tiles and its walls either brick or tile hung. From here the pathway winds through a wilder area called Delos and then back into the Front Courtyard, which can be crossed to enter the Rose Garden.

The Rose Garden is sensational in June and July – a seething mass of perfumed blooms, old shrub roses of the kind that Vita Sackville-West adored, with glorious names like 'Belle de Crecy' and 'Blanc Double de Coubert', underplanted with tobacco plants, Sweet Williams, lavender, and countless other perennials. At its centre is the Yew Rondel – a circular yew hedge cut into four, with views through all four doorways. But walk forwards past the Rondel and look down the next pathway to your left for a dramatic view: a long, narrow alleyway flanked by yews which runs the full length of the garden and has

an urn at the far end. The simple perspective is breathtaking – Harold Nicolson at his best.

Next you can wander through the Cottage Garden which acts as an apron to the South Cottage, the first building restored by the Nicolsons on their arrival. Here are russets and yellows, oranges and reds – the hot colours that would be less comfortable in the Rose Garden. The white rose against the cottage is 'Madame Alfred Carriere'; it was planted on the day the Nicolson's bought Sissinghurst.

'This', says the new guidebook to the garden, 'was the most personal of their gardens. It enfolds memories of their joint lives. Vita would often come down early from her bedroom on the first floor to work in it; and Harold, before he went to London on a Monday morning, would gather flowers from it for his London flat.'

From here a pathway leads through to the Lime Walk, twin pleached *allées* which were Harold's pride and joy but which Vita referred to as 'Platform 5 at Charing Cross'. It would be a mistake to think of Harold

Nicolson as just the designer and not a gardener. Here he was very much 'hands on', referring to the Lime Walk – at its best in spring – as 'MLW' – My Life's Work.

Sissinghurst leaves you with the feeling that you have dined on unparalleled riches. Here are buildings you could die for – the two cottages, the long, low, house and library in mellow brick, and the romantic Elizabethan Tower. They are surrounded by gardens that are cradled in walls of ancient brick and solid rich green yew, and yet within the hard lines are clouds of shrubs and perennials that burst with health and brim over with flowers.

So popular has Sissinghurst become that The National Trust now worries about its ability to cope with the visitors. Timed tickets have already been introduced, so I must encourage you to visit not in the middle of the day, but later in the afternoon when the crowds are abating and the light is softer. It is by far the best time to see the garden here. Sissinghurst between 3 and 5.30pm is perfection, and in either spring or autumn it also has additional charms that the summer coach-loads miss.

Plan your visit to be kind to the garden and so that you can enjoy it at a time of tranquillity. Climb the steps of the tower, as I did, and gaze through the door at the room where Vita Sackville-West wrote *All Passion Spent, Pepita, The Garden* and also her gardening column for *The Observer* for sixteen years. Here she proved herself to be a garden writer of great practicality and enormous sensitivity:

> *Gardener, if you listen, listen well:*
> *Plant for your winter pleasure,*
>   *when the months*
> *Dishearten; plant to find a fragile note*
> *Touched from the brittle violin of frost.* ❧

Some of the ruins of the Tudor house divide up the garden; here the Rose Garden can be seen through the barred window.

INVEREWE
Wester Ross

The key to the successful cultivation of plants here is not just the mild weather – they must be protected from strong winds by tall windbreaks.

Wᴴᴇɴ I ᴡᴀs little we holidayed for a week each year at Bispham, the select end of Blackpool, in Mrs Schofield's boarding house in Hesketh Avenue. Then we had a couple of summers at Butlins, Filey, until mum decided it had 'gone off' and what we needed was a good holiday in the country, with scenery rather than Redcoats to keep us amused. I wasn't too upset. For two years running I'd found it embarrassing entering the 'Mr Debonaire' contest and being unplaced, and my patellae, though sparsely fleshed, were not something I wished to expose in the 'Mr Knobbly Knees' competition. It was decided that next year we would go on a fortnight's motoring holiday to Scotland.

Quite what my parents expected a ten-year-old girl and a fourteen-year-old boy to do for an entire week at Cape Wrath I shall never know, but being from the Yorkshire Dales my sister and I were brought up with a love of moors and tarns which translated well into mountains and lochs, even if Redcoat-style entertainment was thin on the ground.

I have dim memories of that holiday thirty-odd years ago, except those of being

ᴏᴘᴘᴏsɪᴛᴇ *Eucalyptus trees and cabbage palms are not the plants one immediately associates with gardens in Scotland, but then Inverewe is warmed by the Gulf Stream.*

closeted with a grumpy lady watercolourist who was supposed to be giving me painting lessons in Durness, and watching the Queen Mother's equerry, Major Sir Ralph Anstruther Bart, coming down to a breakfast of porridge which he liberally doused with cream. I also remember staying overnight in an Edinburgh boarding house with creaking bedsprings, and in the Royal Hotel in Ullapool, where we enjoyed a really flash meal which, said my dad, had cost more than the previous

three meals that week. Still, they did have a piper in the dining room.

It was on the way to Ullapool that we visited the gardens at Inverewe, and where I encountered a range of plants that I never before knew existed. One solitary hydrangea in the garden at home, along with a few marigolds, a 'Dorothy Perkins' clambering over the fence, and a flowering currant outside the back door had not prepared me for the floral cornucopia that Inverewe presented. Tempered by the North Atlantic Drift – the warm air that started life as the Gulf Stream in the Gulf of Mexico – this garden on the west coast of Scotland is capable of growing a wide range of plants that would be too tender for most other parts of Britain (except Cornwall and the Isles of Scilly, which also benefit from the same airstream).

Not that Inverewe has it easy: salt-laden winds can batter summer flowers into submission in an evening; late frosts can turn rhododendron blooms the colour of toast, and gales can rock the sturdiest of trees. And then, the next morning, the day can be bright and still. In spite of all this, the effects of the North Atlantic Drift, especially in steadying the temperatures of the waters of Loch Ewe, are a great advantage.

It is hard to believe that this was once a treeless piece of windswept coastline, but that was the case when Osgood Hanbury

Mackenzie acquired the land here in 1862. What he did with it is an object lesson in creating a garden in an exposed spot.

Mackenzie was the only son of the second wife of the Laird of Gairloch. At the age of twenty he became the owner of a 12,000-acre Highland estate in Wester Ross which consisted of farms, crofts and crofters, plenty of heathland and a good quantity of bog. He built himself a mansion (a typical Victorian Scottish pile with gables and turrets) on a promontory jutting out into Loch Ewe, and then constructed retaining walls and terraces to create a kitchen garden. Realizing the importance of shelter in this locality, Mackenzie then planted more than one hundred acres of woodland comprising trees that were tough enough to withstand the wind: a hardy Caledonian strain of the Scots pine, Corsican pine, Austrian pine, rowans, alders, birches, beech and oak were all used, and the inhospitable thin, black, peaty soil had to be improved at each planting site with imported earth.

Over the next forty years, until his death in 1922, Osgood Mackenzie hunted, shot, fished and established a fine collection of choice trees and shrubs within his sheltering windbreaks. Alas, his mansion was destroyed by fire in 1914, but the present white-painted house was built on the same site by his daughter, Mairi Sawyer, in 1935. It was Mairi who continued to build up the plant collection and the reputation of Inverewe, until she handed it over to The National Trust for Scotland in 1952, the year before she died.

Today the garden is hugely popular and is even visited by cruise ships which drop off their passengers to spend a day wandering through its rich collection of plants. If you arrive by less sophisticated means – a motor car – you can travel southwards on the A835 from Ullapool, joining the A832 to Poolewe, or travel westwards from Inverness for 84 miles on the same two roads. There aren't a lot of them up here.

When should you visit? Inverewe gets around sixty inches of rain a year. The wettest months are September, October and November, while May and June deliver the most sunshine. Me? I love Scotland in May, before the midges are out and biting. Visit Inverewe in the summer and you'll find midge repellant on offer in the Visitor Centre.

Coming out of the Visitor Centre on your way into the garden you'll have a fine view across the loch and you'll see decorating the gatehouse that wall shrub which always indicates mild weather conditions, *Crinodendron hookerianum*, whose rosy-red bells drip from the branches in late spring.

On the north side of the drive are trees that Osgood Mackenzie planted between 1864 and 1890, including the tough variety of Scots pine he obtained from Loch Maree. They mingle with eucalypts – some of the first that were planted in the British Isles – imported by Osgood from Tasmania in 1880. Tough plants from New Zealand grow beneath them – olearias (of which Inverewe has the National Collection), phormiums, aciphyllas and celmisias, all with sword-like leaves.

Clumps of the palest pink-flowered and hairy-leafed *Rhododendron ciliatum* line the upper path here, which explain why it is called the Ciliatum Walk, and below the drive is the Walled Garden established by Osgood Mackenzie in 1870, its curved beds of earth reputedly imported from Ireland. Today seaweed is regularly hauled up here from the shore to continue improving the soil, and there are borders of perennials, vegetables and cut flowers, along with herbs and tender plants. Pergolas are hung with clematis and roses, and at the eastern end of the garden are greenhouses that shelter bromeliads and other exotics.

One of the enduring images of Inverewe is of the white-painted house with its pale grey slate roof. Surrounded by sheltering trees, it comes after the Walled Garden and looks out over a lawn which has a broad herbaceous border around its top edge and a dramatic rock garden running down to the shores of Loch Ewe. Mairi Sawyer began this feature which has

In front of the white-painted house are broad herbaceous borders, fronted by a lawn and rock banks that slope towards Loch Ewe.

As you walk around Inverewe you'll find that you're reminded, every now and then, of its situation, with views of Loch Ewe and the distant mountains coming into sight.

since been extended, and it is now home to a wonderful mixture of plants from Asia, Europe and Australasia. New Zealand plants seem to love it here, as do many from the Mediterranean.

Now the choices become more difficult. Paths take off to left and right, one leading through 'Japan'. Here in the wild wood-land are hostas and ferns, the Chusan palm (*Trachycarpus fortunei*) and a grove of tree ferns, *Dicksonia antarctica*.

You will see wonderful banks of primulas and astilbes, and Petiolarid primulas from the Himalayas that gar-deners down south can only dream of.

Rocky banks appear now, supporting shade-loving plants, leading to the Wet Valley, where a calm pool is positively sheeted with water lilies.

This is an adventure that would appeal to anyone, even a fourteen-year-old boy and his ten-year-old sister. No wonder we loved it. Palmate newts thrive here, as do gigantic gunneras and rodgersias.

Eventually you'll make your way upwards to Am Ploc Ard – Gaelic for 'The High Lump' (but roughly translated as 'High Viewpoint'). There is no denying it, the High Lump offers wonderful views of the chilly blue waters of Loch Ewe and Poolewe village across to the Torridon Hills, a pale purplish grey on the day of my last visit. To the north, on a clear day, you might just see the Outer Hebrides. These

are views that bring to your ears the strains of 'Fingal's Cave' and 'The Land of the Mountain and the Flood', as you double back from Am Ploc Ard and wander on down the steep paths of the Devil's Elbow with its Sikkim rhododendrons. You could be in the Himalayan foothills.

And so the adventure continues, up and down paths that lead you to the jetty on Camas Glas, where you can sit quietly and watch the water for signs of otters and seals, or perhaps through woodland embellished with the ethereal flowers of the blue meconopsis.

Blackcaps and whitethroats flit among the branches. This is the country of golden eagle and merlin, of red deer and pine marten. They have been a part of this landscape even longer than Osgood Mackenzie and Mairi Sawyer's garden, and along with Inverewe they are probably responsible for the fact that my sister and I have always preferred the wilder parts of Britain to Butlins. ❧

The Walled Garden is the first thing most visitors see on their arrival – stuffed with vegetables, fruits and flowering plants. Seaweed provides soil enrichment.

CASTLE HOWARD
North Yorkshire

Alan Ayckbourn is a brilliant playwright, but it is difficult to imagine him designing a stately home. The same applies to Sir John Vanbrugh. And yet, with the restoration comedies *The Relapse* and *The Provok'd Wife* behind him, he turned from drama to architecture and designed a house for his pal at the Kit-Cat Club, Charles, 3rd Earl of Carlisle.

You'd have thought a chap might have started with a semi. Unbelievably, Castle Howard was Vanbrugh's first commission. Until then he was, as the guidebook indelicately puts it, 'an architectural virgin'. Vanbrugh refused to let this stand in his way and if he did not know everything himself, he knew a man who did. He consulted the accomplished architect Nicholas Hawksmoor on practical matters, and building began around 1700 with Vanbrugh providing the imagination and Hawksmoor the experience. The Earl, the architect and the playwright also designed the original layout of the grounds. The west wing of the house was added after Vanbrugh's death.

OPPOSITE The Atlas Fountain, with its spume rising up into the air, is a perfect complement to the south front of Castle Howard. Atlas was brought here from the Great Exhibition in 1851 and the mermen who squirt him with water arrived by steam train shortly afterwards.

Disaster struck in 1940 when a raging fire destroyed much of the south wing, including the dome. Restoration followed and Castle Howard remains one of the finest houses in Britain with a setting that is second to none.

Even the entrance to the estate is theatrical. It is signposted off the York to Scarborough road, just before you reach Malton. At first the country lane is flanked by oaks and ashes and then a strange monument appears on your left – a tallish column with something battered on the top. It used to be a lamp says the guidebook. The broken standard lamp is surrounded by smaller columns, each bearing a visored head. The whole thing was apparently erected by public subscription in 1869 to the 7th Earl of Carlisle who 'by his public conduct won the respect of his country'. We don't seem to erect standard lamps for public conduct any more.

After the lamp the road becomes straight as a die and slopes downwards, then upwards. Across it at the bottom of the valley is a stone archway with a castellated wall to either side and a tower at each end. There are cross-shaped arrow slits in each tower and, again, the tops are castellated, making this look like the entrance to a medieval fortress. This is Hawksmoor's Carrmire Gate. You'll pass

under the archway, discovering more farmland to right and left, and then the straight road rises towards another gateway, this time with a vast stone pyramid on its top and buildings of

The Rose Gardens are a very special feature at Castle Howard. They are visited every year by many thousands of people, some of whom make an annual pilgrimage to enjoy the spectacular show of colour and perfume.

sandstone to either side. This is Vanbrugh's Curtain Wall – an elaborate creation incorporating eleven different towers. There is no mistaking the fact that you are going somewhere important.

After you have passed beneath the pyramid it is downhill again. Ahead of you there is a towering obelisk. You'll find monument after monument on this road, but this one-hundred-foot obelisk, dating from 1714, acts as a roundabout. Turn off here into the car park with, as yet, no view of the house.

The day is a summer classic. It's warm, the sky is blue and echoing with birdsong, and there are fluffy white clouds. If you had to pick a day to see a house and gardens, then this is the sort of day you'd pick. It is half past three in the afternoon, but the gardens stay open in summer until half past six, so there's no rush.

I leave the car and walk through the entrance gates to the stable yard . A shop occupies one corner of the pale honey-coloured buildings, Jorvik Glass occupies another, and a café a third corner. The entrance to the gardens is in the fourth corner, through smart automatic glass

doors. No hansom cab or coach and pair ever passed through these!

Outside the stable block on the other side a yellow tractor thunders up. Behind it are two trailers fitted with seats and covered with pennant-bedecked awnings, rather like medieval jousting tents on wheels – a sort of Camelot meets Massey Ferguson. This machine will take you to the house if you can't bear to walk. I can, and head off through the high brick wall ahead of me into the first port of call – the Rose Gardens.

The border on the other side of the wall is planted up with modern 'English roses' – varieties that have been raised in recent years by David Austin. Here you will find 'Swan' and 'The Prioress', 'Charles Austin' and many more. The broad, straight path is of grass and there is a yew hedge to the right – it's like walking down a narrow alley with roses to the left, followed by beds of lilies and agapanthus, and greenery to the right. Tantalizingly, at the end of the wall, you can see the rooftops of the castle but, as yet, nothing more.

Then comes a right turn and you can enter the Rose Gardens proper – four

of them within the sheltered confines of this high wall. But first come delphinium borders surrounding two raised beds criss-crossed with box and planted up with antirrhinums.

Enter the doorway to the Rose Gardens and drink in the fragrance of old shrub roses and modern hybrid teas, lavender and clove pinks. Most of the beds are wisely underplanted with all manner of border perennials and herbs that complement the roses, in both sight and fragrance, and mask the grey dust that would otherwise surround them.

There is a pool and a fountain, a boy with a dolphin, box edging and trellis pyramids covered with roses. An arbour is draped with 'Albertine', and there is a wondrous hornbeam hedge on stilts around the Head Gardener's cottage – the smallest house that Sir John Vanbrugh ever designed. An oak pergola supports more climbers, and ramblers have been trained through the branches of old apple trees. In late June and well into July this is a place to lose yourself. You can drown in the perfume.

The four Rose Gardens here have different names, but the planting is so rich and lush that they seem to merge into one another beneath the high brick walls, built in 1706. They were originally used to shelter grapes, figs and pineapples for which Castle Howard became famous, and it was not until the 1970s that they were planted with roses. Lady Cecilia's Garden is now in its prime, but the Venus and Sundial Gardens have recently been replanted as they suffered a bout of rose sickness and the soil had to be replaced to a couple of feet in depth.

The delphinium borders at Castle Howard are at their best in July when the towering spires of these reliable perennials open their flowers of white, purple, and pale or dark blue. The stout canes and tall hedging help to protect them from wind damage.

Lady Cecilia was the wife of George Howard, one-time Chairman of the BBC and later Lord Howard of Henderskelfe, who lived in Castle Howard for nigh on forty years. I planted a tree with him once, while photographers snapped away, to celebrate fifty years of gardening at the BBC. He was not a slim man, and I remember having difficulty getting my foot into the hole to firm back the soil at the same time as his. He was a snappy dresser. He wore a blue suit with white flecks in it; looking up at him was like looking up at the night sky. George Howard was a colourful man of great vision and energy who presided over the restoration of Castle Howard after the fire. It's due to him that the dome, destroyed in the blaze, was replaced in 1960. He died in 1984 and the estate is now administered by his four sons. His gilded initials are woven into the wrought-iron gate through which you leave the Rose Gardens and head towards the house.

Turn left, underneath avenues of enormous lime trees, and walk towards what you just know is going to be a stupendous view. The ground rises a little ahead of you and then falls away. People are standing on the knoll looking out ahead of them as though they are on the prow of a ship. Join them and gaze at the landscape that unfolds in front of you – the Howardian Hills make a backdrop for the silvered lake, the emerald fields, the fuzzy woodland, and the drystone walls that furnish the Dales of North Yorkshire. To your right is the jewel in the crown – Castle Howard itself.

Its sandstone is the colour of honey and it is capped by a great lantern dome. Peacocks strut about the wide steps that lead up to every entrance, and their shrieks echo across the valley on the still, warm air. On the house's north front the ground slopes down to the lake. On its south front is a long, broad lawn centred by the Atlas Fountain – a massive waterwork with a

crouching Atlas carrying on his shoulders a copper globe banded with the signs of the zodiac. Poor chap, I'm sure he has enough on his mind without having to cope with the four mermen squirting water at him from cornucopia-like shells.

I first came here in my Uncle Bert's Dormobile in the late 1950s, with my Mum and Dad, Uncle Bert and Auntie Edie. The engine overheated in the traffic jams at York and we had to lift the cover between the front seats to let it cool off. It was my first visit to a stately home, and the Atlas Fountain is the thing I remember above all else. That and the weather. The day was warm and sunny, very much like today, and I walked along in the shade of the seemingly gigantic yew hedges.

Around the fountain the eight-foot hedges of yew have replaced the elaborate parterres of William Nesfield who added to the Pleasure Grounds in the 1850s. They were done away with in the 1890s by the 9th Countess and the simpler scheme installed. Other pieces of Nesfield's handiwork have survived – the Prince

Like all good rose gardens, those at Castle Howard are planted up not just with roses but with a richly varied collection of ground-cover plants. These will complement the blooms above – everything from herbs to dwarf pinks and violas – extending the season of fragrance as well as colour.

of Wales Fountain, with its fleur-de-lis of water jets, lies next to the Atlas Fountain. It was thought to have a single jet until the lake was dredged in 1986 and the cast-iron fountain-head for the subsidiary jets was found. They unclogged it, fitted it back, turned it on, and up rose the Prince of Wales Feathers.

The fountain operates on Sundays and Bank Holidays, along with the Cascade and Waterfall which draw your eye to the imposing Mausoleum on the far hills. Here rest the heads of the family beneath Hawksmoor's dome, which catches the last coppery rays of the sun each evening.

The pathway along the south side of the house leads you past borders planted up with peonies, lupins, sweet peas,

The south front reveals the grandeur of Sir John Vanbrugh's design for Castle Howard. The dome, destroyed by fire in 1940, was replaced in 1960 under the tenure of George Howard.

Because of rose sickness the soil in the Venus and Sundial Gardens was completely replaced. It was a mammoth task to completely replace 22,000 cubic feet of soil and not damage the surrounding lawns. The hard work has paid off and the new plants are in good health.

irises and other perennials, all towered over by a blue-faced clock with gilded numerals. The pathway rises now towards Vanbrugh's Palladian-style Temple of the Four Winds, approached up a grassy hill that was once the main street of the village of Henderskelfe. From the Temple's mound there are more breathtaking views over the Yorkshire Dales. Down below is the river and its dainty three-arched sandstone bridge.

But for gardeners and plantsmen the greatest pleasure comes in a walk from the Temple into Ray Wood, a tract of English woodland which has tree surveys dating back to 1563. It has since been added to with all manner of exotic trees and

shrubs, from eight hundred species of rhododendrons and azaleas to pieris, acers, bamboos and roses. It was the brainchild of Jim Russell, for many years head plants-man here after he left the family firm of Sunningdale Nurseries in Berkshire. He brought with him many rare and choice plants, some of whose ancestors were collected by Hooker, Farrer and Kingdon-Ward. Over fourteen hundred rhododendron plants were brought here in the late sixties, and major planting took place in the 1970s. Booklets are available detailing spring, summer and autumn walks through Ray Wood, and there are helpful coloured arrows to keep you on the right tracks.

Keen gardeners will spend hours in here. The planting is spectacular yet sensitive, and not what Castle Howard's horticulturist Lin Hawthorne calls 'Kurumi-hell – the Brentford Nylons of horticulture'. Indeed, some of the larger-leafed rhododendrons are exceptionally

choice, thriving in the leafy soil beneath the raised canopy of oak trees in a garden which has surprisingly low rainfall for the north of England.

Jim Russell's legacy is being added to with the creation of an important new arboretum, not due to be opened to the public for another ten years or so. When it is finally revealed it should provide further incentive for plantsmen to visit Castle Howard.

Lin walks with me up the slope towards Ray Wood and then leaves me to explore. Already most folk are wending their way home, but it is only five o'clock and the best part of the day is yet to come. A great sense of tranquillity descends on the garden in the early evening as I amble up and down the paths that weave through the wood. You'll find surprises and delights at every turn whatever the season. You'll even be able to find peace and quiet in high summer. It is, says Lin, the closest most of us get to the Himalayas.

Down through the woodland I dawdle, beneath oaks and pines, past banks of moss and tufts of ferns, and under the canopies of spruces, pines, oaks and birches, to the shores of the enormous lake. A long, low, cream-painted café with orangery windows and lollipop bay trees in tubs sits right on the waterline. Waves lap at the wooden supports of its jetty, where an electric boat has plied back and forth all day, and where visitors have sat and enjoyed their tea. Now it is deserted, and in the warm June sun, with haze rising from the water, I could be on the shores of Lake Maggiore, except that the hills beyond the twinkling water are those of Yorkshire, not Italy. It's hard to believe that no one else is here to enjoy this bit of heaven, but then it's half past five and the coach loads are probably on their way to Harry Ramsden's.

I walk back towards the house now as the sun catches the top of the distant Mausoleum. The Rose Gardens, which earlier were full of tourists, are now mine alone and, if possible, even more fragrant than before. It is a scene that fires the imagination. The atmosphere is so rich and evocative that you can see why it attracted the producers of the televised version of Waugh's *Brideshead Revisited*.

The effect of the television series is not so transitory as you might imagine. It helped pay for the restoration of many of the rooms on the south front, including the Garden Hall, where new murals by Felix Kelly replace those by Pellegrini which are lost forever.

As I left Castle Howard, driving northwards towards the Howardian Hills

with the stone of the house glowing gold in the evening sun, I tried to remember the words of Charles Ryder in Waugh's novel. I failed. When I got home I looked them up:

'I had been there before; first with Sebastian more than twenty years ago on a cloudless day in June, when the ditches were creamy with meadowsweet and the air heavy with all the scents of summer; it was a day of peculiar splendour, and though I had been there so often, in so many moods, it was to that first visit that my heart returned on this, my latest.'

But there was no mention of a Dormobile.

The grassy hill which leads to the Temple of the Four Winds was once the main street of the village of Henderskelfe. The view from the temple is quite breathtaking. You can look down over the river (a tributary of the Derwent) and its three-arched sandstone bridge, and then over to the Yorkshire hills and dales beyond.

1 LISTER ROAD

London

LEYTONSTONE. NOT EXACTLY on the Equator. Not exactly opulent in terms of greenery, you might think. But there's one corner of Leytonstone that comes as near to the tropical rain forest as any garden I've ever seen, and that's Myles Challis's garden in Lister Road.

Now if you were told that you were about to visit a garden that felt like a jungle, you'd probably expect something on the grand scale. But the garden at Lister Road is tiny, just twenty feet by forty feet, though when you enter it you feel like you're entering another world.

The garden itself began life ten years ago, but Myles' interest in things that grew developed much earlier.

'I was taken to Kew when I was seven years old. There was a house called the Aroid House. It was full of all these wonderful, huge, tropical, big-leaved plants. Of course at seven years old I was not very high. And that was it. Something went 'ping' and I thought "this is wonderful."'

'I had an uncle who was a tropical butterfly collector, so I said "Right; from

OPPOSITE *The foliage mixture in Myles Challis's garden is of incomparable richness. Bamboos and eucalyptuses act as a backdrop to the larger, broader leaves of paulownia and rodgersia, gunnera and castor oil plant to create a lush, tropical effect.*

The Kahili ginger, Hedychium gardnerianum, *pushes up its cockades of yellow flowers in summer. More frequently seen in the Mediterranean or the Caribbean, it is of borderline hardiness here.*

now on, when you are in Java or Borneo or wherever, you can dig me up a few bits and pieces and send them back", which he did. So about twice a year a big wooden crate would arrive from literally anywhere, packed with all these bulbs and cuttings and things all wrapped in moss. Within the space of only a few years I had this amazing collection of tropical plants growing in my parents' conservatory.'

Myles became something of a child prodigy where the cultivation of exotics was concerned. He was thirteen when he staged his first exhibit at the Hampstead Horticultural Society's Great Autumn Show in the town hall. 'It sort of knocked everyone senseless because they'd never seen most of these plants before.'

But disaster was to befall this unique collection. The oil crisis of the late seventies sent fuel prices rocketing and young Myles was told by his father that they could no longer afford to heat the conservatory at their Hampstead home. Some of the plants were sold, some were given to Kew and various other botanical institutions, and Myles was at a loss as to what to do. He just carried on reading about the plants he loved – anything with big leaves.

He found that not all plants with large leaves – gunnera for instance – needed the protection of a greenhouse to get them through the winter, so he started growing those, initially in his parents' garden and then later, when he moved away, in his own gardens – culminating in number 1 Lister Road.

Gunnera, bamboos, the Chusan palm (*Trachycarpus fortunei*) and eucalyptuses came first; plants that Myles describes as 'very ordinary things'. Then he came upon *A Gloucestershire Wild Garden*, a book describing a surgeon general's attempts to grow in England the exotic plants he had seen in India, and he thought: 'my God; you can have a really exotic-looking garden outside. You don't have to garden under glass to make this really lush, exotic, wonderful effect.' And that's when he really got hooked and started going for the exotics in a big way.

He admits that this is really a reincarnation of the Victorian craze for subtropical gardening which has been totally abandoned for the best part of this century. The thing that still astounds him is why few other gardeners had cottoned on to the technique until his own exhibit at the Chelsea Flower Show in 1986 captured their imagination.

I can remember it myself. A head-and-shoulders statue of Neptune, trident in hand, spurted water from his mouth into a pool. He emerged from a grassy bank and was surrounded by foliar grandeur. People stopped in their tracks, unaware that plants like these could thrive in the open air.

The exhibit made Myles Challis's name. He was amazed by the reaction of both the press and the public. He'd made the statue himself from chicken wire and cement, based on a lump of Bernini statuary he'd seen in the Victoria and Albert Museum. Today it resides in a mill pond on a farm in Dunmow, in Essex, and at the bottom of the garden at 1 Lister Road is another lump of Challis statuary – a three-foot-high mask of Apollo which squirts water into a shallow pool. At the edges of the pool grow massive parasols of gunnera and great paddle-shaped leaves of lysichiton, but these have to be reached by walking through the rest of the plants in the garden. Well, you don't walk through them really, you walk under them.

You enter the gate and swish aside the fronds of the Chusan palm, before parting the stems of a gigantic bamboo and ducking underneath the overhanging branches

of a eucalyptus. All around you are plants that make you feel small. There is a large-leafed poplar, *Populus lasiocarpa*, and *Magnolia delavayi*, the evergreen magnolia with flower buds like fat cigars.

Large pots stand among the tall stems of these trees, containing daturas and Abyssinian bananas. At the back – for you have to look closely to see everything that grows here – is a fence cloaked in the evergreen *Clematis armandii* and *Parthenocissus henryana*, woven together like some thick tweed coat.

Ginger lilies (hedychiums) and ligularias, purple-leafed cannas and grey-

The entrance to this tiny garden immediately transports you to a tropical jungle. As you follow the winding path you'll have to duck beneath the fronds of tree ferns, the sword-like leaves of New Zealand flax, and the fleshy leaves of cannas.

leafed *Melianthus major* form the undergrowth in a garden that you have to keep telling yourself is less than half the size of a tennis court.

He works with really fast-growing plants that have huge leaves and can be heavily pruned. Things like the foxglove tree, *Paulownia tomentosa*, which has downy leaves that are easily as big as tea trays, and the rice-paper plant, *Tetrapanax papyrifer*, which has even hairier leaves that are fingered and held on the ends of long leaf stalks.

What these fast-growing, large-leafed plants need is plenty of food and water. The garden is watered with a hosepipe every other day in summer, and fed with liquid manure once a week. Concentrated animal manure is dissolved in water and then diluted and applied to the earth around these greedy monsters.

Many of the plants Myles uses are 'root hardy' – they will be killed to ground level by frosts in winter, but will regenerate from the rootstock come the spring. He helps them make it through the cold weather by mounding up builders' aggregate (a mixture of sharp sand and gravel) around the rootstocks of those that are a bit on the tender side.

Pot plants like bananas and datura are lugged through the hedge on one side of the garden in autumn and overwintered in the neighbour's greenhouse.

But most of the plants are pretty tough. The black-stemmed bamboo, *Phyllostachys nigra*, shoots up by the fence (if you could see the fence) at the right-hand-side of the garden, and there is a wonderful clump on the left of a golden-green stemmed bamboo, *Semiarundinaria fastuosa*, which grows to a height of about fifteen feet, but which spreads sideways only very slowly, making it suitable for small gardens where height but not invasiveness is wanted.

In the shade cast by the poplar and the eucalyptus grows a tree fern – *Dicksonia antarctica* – from Tasmania. The Tasmanian tree ferns are more hardy in British gardens than those from Australia, and nowadays they are readily available.

After ten years the garden is more than bursting at the seams. How long will he stay at Lister Road? With half his working week spent in Newbury and the other half in Tunbridge Wells, he feels that to live in Leytonstone is perhaps not the most convenient location.

What, I wonder, will those who next live in the house think of their garden? And how will the estate agent describe it in his blurb about the house? It goes against the grain for any agent to describe a garden as 'a jungle', but in this case, for once, he would be right. I hope he doesn't simply settle for 'established'.

Myles Challis has created the most wonderful escape from the traffic and stress of the city by letting visitors into this tiny patch of paradise. His garden has been open by appointment for the last few years and one day three hundred people came round in an afternoon. Quite how they got in, and quite what they made of it, I don't know. But they can't fail to have been won over by this technique of gardening, and to have gone away thinking that they must try and make their own bit of tropical rain forest in Purley, or Blackburn, or Macclesfield or Blandford Forum. I know I did. This sort of gardening is contagious. ❧

Among other plants that are permanently established in the garden – including the blue-grey Melianthus major *– are more tender subjects which stand out in pots during the summer; plants like datura, or angel's trumpet, which releases an aniseed fragrance after sunset.*

SNOWSHILL MANOR

Gloucestershire

COTSWOLD VILLAGES FILL me with unease. Broadway more than most. The problem is excessive beauty. Each honeyed cottage and villa is more perfect than the last. A stroll down Broadway's main street leaves me feeling that I have dined for too long on rich food. Windows are mullioned, gardens are walled; around every corner is a view that Americans would die for.

Am I jaded? Am I jaundiced? No. There are delights to be had in the Cotswolds simply by turning your car off the beaten tourist track. When you have feasted your eyes on antique shops and designer woollens, the classy Lygon Arms and executive emporia, turn south at the end of Broadway's main street and follow the signs to Snowshill Manor. You are about to escape into another world, unless you make the mistake of coming here on a Sunday or Bank Holiday Monday, when the place might be heaving. The National Trust knows this, and so in 1995 they

OPPOSITE *The garden at Snowshill Manor falls away down the slope towards the bottom of the valley. A rich selection of climbing roses and trained fruit trees decorates its outer wall.*

opened new visitor facilities (including car park, shop and restaurant) just outside the village on the Broadway road. The route to the manor from here avoids the main street, but the approach through the orchard is quite steep.

Alternatively, at the foot of the village of Snowshill leave your car in the grass and gravel car park and walk up and then down the hill to Snowshill Manor. Here you'll pass cottages that have hollyhocks outside their front doors. You'll also have your first sighting of blue paint. 'Wade Blue' paint – a mixture of azure and turquoise rather lighter than that at nearby Hidcote. The man after whom the paint is named is Charles Paget Wade, who bought Snowshill Manor in 1919 and surrounded it with a garden that I reckon to be one of the most delightful in the country.

Wade was born in 1883 and had a solitary childhood, especially at the age of seven when he was sent to live with his grandmother in Great Yarmouth. On Sundays his grandmother would open her Chinese cabinet in the drawing room and let the young Charles Wade feast his eyes on the peculiar treasures it contained – musical boxes, a wax angel, a bone model

of a spinning wheel and much more. He would comb the seashore and was as fascinated with the 'wrought-iron nails in the tarred wooden pier' as with the Punch and Judy show.

His delight in form and texture led him to become an artist and architect, and a legacy allowed him to purchase Snowshill Manor when he saw it advertised in

White doves strut about the mellow stone roof of the dovecot which is now a potting shed.

Country Life. It was once owned by Henry VIII, and later passed on to Catherine Parr, his surviving wife. The manor's oldest surviving portion dates back to 1500.

It was a near derelict farm when Wade bought it, but in the years that followed he filled the house with an amazing collection of artefacts that reflected his love of the arts and crafts movement. Today the sturdy L-shaped house is a collection of strangely named rooms: Meridian and Zenith, Admiral and Hundred Wheels, the former filled with nautical memorabilia and the latter with boneshaker bicycles. Samurai armour can be found – twenty-six suits of it – and a room called Mizzen is filled with cloth-making equipment. It was not necessarily expensive things that caught the imagination of Charles Wade, but things that were well made and which fulfilled William Morris's dictum that you should have nothing in your house that was not beautiful or useful.

As you walk down the garden at Snowshill, turn to look back at the Cotswold stone house that sits above it.

The guidebook shows several pictures of Wade – an Oscar Wilde like figure standing on the steps of his house clad in Cromwellian armour, his flowing locks centrally parted. It's heartening to know that in later years he sat by the fire in the Priest's House listening to *Much Binding in the Marsh* on his battery operated radio. Wade died in 1956 and is buried in Snowshill churchyard. He handed over the house and its collection of artefacts to The National Trust so that folk could marvel

Looking out from the top terrace of the garden you will gaze down on to a lawn, in the centre of which is a gilded armillary sundial set on top of a tall stone column.

---

at the diversity of its treasures. But then, as Queen Mary remarked after visiting Snowshill, 'the most notable part of the collection was Mr Wade himself.'

Today the house and its contents are on view, and you cannot fail to be fascinated by the cornucopia of craftsmanship. But the garden; ah, the garden. Walk through the entrance gate under a canopy of towering trees. The handsome house stands before you at the end of a gravel path, but where is the garden?

Turn left at the house and you have a tantalizing glimpse of it behind a tall, lichen-encrusted wall. The wall runs downhill and rising beyond it is the Gloucestershire countryside. I was here in the first week of September when the sky is a clear forget-me-not blue and the rolling hills are straw coloured, or rich green and dotted with sheep. Every knoll is crowned with trees and only the occasional jet fighter breaks the spell. Birdsong echoes from the woodland, and to the left of the buff-coloured path beside the wall a white cat rolls in lush green grass beneath an orchard of elderberries.

The wall, ten feet tall, is smothered in a welter of vines and figs, espalier apples and pears. At its foot is a border of perennials – penstemons and poppies, lavender and roses – and in it a doorway is crowned with the legend:

A GARDYN WALLED AL WITH
STOON
SO FAIR A GARDYN WOT I
NOWHERE NOON

Pass through the doorway to a stone-flagged courtyard. On the wall of the building opposite is a gilded statue of St George slaying the dragon. Once he struck the bell that hangs above him.

Now turn left and you begin to sense the atmosphere of the garden as the valley falls away before you. A series of terraces descends from the house, some of them incorporating the old stone outbuildings – from cow-shed to dovecot – each of them with its own character. The garden at Snowshill, like that at Hidcote Manor, is a series of rooms or enclosures. But Hidcote is grander and more formal while Snowshill retains something of the more friendly farmyard atmosphere.

From the top terrace you can look over a rectangular lawn with a central armillary sundial; its gilded sphere shines in the sun. On one wall is a complicated looking clock. It is a nychthemeron, a twenty-four-hour clock designed by Charles Wade to show the time of day and the month and with the appropriate sign of the zodiac.

The most surprising thing about this garden is that, in spite of Wade being an architect, he did not design it by himself. He commissioned MH Baillie Scott, a great exponent of the Arts and Crafts Movement, to produce some designs which he then adapted and brought to life. Wade had firm ideas on gardens: 'A garden is an extension of the house, a series of outdoor rooms. The word garden means a garth, an enclosed space. So the design was planned as a series of separate courts,

sunny ones contrasting with shady ones and different courts for varying moods.

'The plan of the garden is much more important than the flowers in it.

'Mystery is most valuable in design; never show all there is at once. Plan for enticing vistas with a hint of something beyond.'

Wade's garden lives up to his maxims, and also to Goethe's observation that 'English gardens are not made to a plan but from a feeling heart.' Well, the better ones anyway.

The garden does hold the surprises that Wade felt were so important. At every turn there is a enticing glimpse of something new. A deep rectangular pool, benches and tubs in that azure livery, a shady guelder rose walk terminating in a view to the west across the Cotswold Hills, a mask of Bacchus dribbling water into a lead cistern, or a wicket gate to an orchard in which an old wooden wheelbarrow leans into a heap beneath the pippins.

The paintwork at Snowshill Manor is of a colour named after its owner – Wade Blue. It is a rich livery that contrasts well with the pale ochre of Cotswold stone.

White doves coo and flap atop the stone dovecot, which is now a potting shed, and swags of *Vitis coignetiae* hang like an arras over its door. On the wall is an engraved tablet:

HOURS FLY
FLOWERS DIE
NEW DAYS
NEW WAYS
PASS BY
LOVE STAYS

The garden at Snowshill Manor is barely two acres, but within its confines are sunlight and shadows, cool shade, the dripping of water, the rustling of leaves and the intrigue its creator believed was essential in 'outdoor rooms'.

The final words about this garden must be those that Wade himself thought appropriate: "Tis man's rest, children's fairyland, birds' orchestra, butterfly's banquet; a place for pretty thoughts and soft musings, with summer reveries, moonlight ecstasies, love's occasion, youth's yearning... Here be delights that will fetch the day about from sun to sun, and rock the tedious year as in a delightful dream.'

STUDLEY ROYAL

North Yorkshire

It has taken me some considerable time and a lot of serious thinking – there are, after all, a number of options. Being faced with the challenge of disposing of at least eight million pounds is quite some responsibility and not a decision to be made hastily. But I have, at last, come up with a master plan. Some of the money will go to charity, but I shall keep enough back to build the most dramatic garden created in living memory. I will become the John Aislabie of the twenty-first century – when I win the National Lottery.

Aislabie was Tory Member of Parliament for Ripon. He inherited the Studley Estate in 1693 and fulfilled his great political ambitions by becoming Chancellor of the Exchequer in 1718. He began to develop that part of the estate which formed a wooded valley on the banks of the River Skell.

But disaster struck. Aislabie was deeply involved in the South Sea Company scheme – a company which had the British monopoly on trade with South America and the Pacific islands. Aislabie himself promoted the bill in Parliament. It was a

wizard scheme which made pots of money for its investors when things were going well. In fact things went so well that the company's sole purpose was to pay the National Debt in return for further concessions. It all gets a bit complicated for me from here on in. Anyway, we're talking Lloyds. It all went wrong. Very wrong. Bogus companies tried to get in on the act. Huge success was followed by total collapse – 'The South Sea Bubble' burst and Aislabie was expelled from Parliament after being found guilty of the 'most notorious, dangerous and infamous corruption'. He was thrown into the Tower of London and disqualified from public office for life. Totally fed up he came home and gardened. I am glad he did – Studley Royal is the result.

Mind you, Aislabie must have had some money left to carry out the construction of the now famous Water Gardens. They lead the visitor upriver to the ruins of Fountains Abbey, purchased by Aislabie's son, William, after his father's death in 1742. Both father and son share the responsibility for creating a landscape which is considered to be the finest eighteenth-century water garden in England.

Thankfully fate decreed that the formal areas should escape the worst ravages of the 'natural movement' of the late eighteenth century which swept away many intricate

High on a hill, overlooking the Temple of Piety, is the Banqueting House. From here you'll have tantalizing glimpses of the water features below, through a tracery of foliage provided by the trees on the slopes of the valley.

schemes and replaced them with more rugged landscapes. Much of the Studley Royal landscape is, indeed, romantic and natural looking thanks to William Aislabie, but his father's formal creation is at its heart.

This is not a flower garden, but a garden composed of green lawns that divide up sheets of water, and a romantic tree-filled landscape with carefully placed

OPPOSITE Of all the ornamental buildings at Studley Royal, the classical Temple of Piety has the finest setting. Its reflection can be seen in a large circular pool of water and it is backed by a steep hill furnished with gigantic beech trees.

From the Octagon Tower you'll have one of the best views of the pools and canals at Studley Royal and you'll see right across to the other side of the valley. The Banqueting House is set high on the opposite hill.

follies and statuary. The Water Garden occupies 150 of the 900 acres which today make up the estate. But there is no house. It was ravaged by fire in 1946 and subsequently pulled down – today only the

imposing stable block remains in the park, along with the amazing St Mary's Church, which was designed for the man who succeeded to the estate in 1859 – the Marquess of Ripon, later Viceroy of India. Regarded as the architect William Burges's religious masterpiece, St Mary's was completed in 1878 and is a real gothic delight. Its interior has to be seen to be believed – deliciously over the top, a feast of gilt and elaborate ornamentation. You'll

pass it on the road which constitutes the entrance to Fountain's Abbey.

The Studley Royal estate was handed down through the family, but eventually came under the control of the West Riding County Council in 1966, to be taken over by The National Trust in 1983. It is the Trust who are now restoring those parts of the estate which need repair, and who are ensuring that it remains the greatest water garden of its time.

The important thing when you visit Studley Royal is to approach it from the lake end and not the Fountains Abbey end. That way its treasures are revealed in the right order, with Fountains Abbey coming as a grand finale.

Out of Ripon, on the Pateley Bridge road, the countryside is classic soft Yorkshire – not the high and rugged fells of hard Yorkshire, but gently rolling hills and dales, with cows grazing in meadows and woodlands occupying smooth-contoured hills like rich green fleece.

Take the turn to the left signposted to Studley Roger. You will eventually skirt the rim of a wide lake with a cascade tipping water into its far end between two square stone pavilions – the fishing tabernacles. Park your car in the car park at this entrance and enter alongside the café at the Canal Gates.

Now it's only fair to warn you that you are in for a long walk if you undertake the full Titchmarsh tour, so avail yourself of the fresh egg-and-cress sandwiches and flapjack of the tearoom (home-made and the best you'll find) before setting out on this adventure. Climb the path ahead of you and, to your left, the Water Gardens begin to appear. There is a long canal and beyond it a circular pool – the Moon Pool – flanked by two crescent shaped pools. Beyond them is a classical temple – the Temple of Piety – and above them, at the top of a precipitous knoll, is the Octagon Tower with spiky finials at its corners. A path winds up to the right now. Climb this to admire the Banqueting House you will find at the top – a handsome structure designed by Colen Campbell – and look through the trees at the tantalizing snatches of water that appear below, culminating in a dramatic view of the long canal with a cascade at its end.

The pathway winds down again, taking you along the canal to the cascade at its top, and then you can turn left and come back down the other side of the pools to take a closer look at the Temple of Piety and enjoy the sheer scale of Studley Royal, constructed before the days of the JCB and utilising a local labour force of a hundred men. Aislabie employed a local man, John Simpson, to oversee the works and, according to Simpson, everything was

The Cascade falls from beneath a rustic stone bridge to fill up the long canal. It was built in the 1730s, at the same time as the nearby grotto, during a period when rusticity was highly fashionable.

worked out by trial and error on site. Simpson's health broke down under the strain and, in 1728, he was succeeded by a master mason called Robert Doe from London. William Fisher was Aislabie's head gardener. Between them they completed the first phase of construction by 1730, levelling the valley floor, turning the river into a canal and excavating the Half Moon Pond above it to feed the cascade. Tent Hill, above Half Moon Pond was also constructed. It's all mind boggling when you consider the lack of mechanisation two and a half centuries ago. This is landscaping on a grand scale.

The design of the formal part of the garden owes much to the influence of the creator of Versailles – André Le Nôtre – and to Queen Anne's gardeners, London and Wise. The buildings were added as eye-catchers once the main scheme was complete, and the statuary followed in the 1730s – all but one are of lead, and were made by Andries Carpentière, a Flemish

sculptor whose work can also be found at Powis Castle.

The pools in front of the Temple of Piety are speckled with water lilies, but you turn right and leave them behind you just after the temple, to head up through the woods beneath mighty beech trees and yews to the Octagon Tower. Panting, you'll pass rocky outcrops in the cool and mossy-scented dimness as the pools slip further below. Eventually you'll come to a dark tunnel, with no light at the end. Be brave – go in. It snakes round to the right, the light appears and you are deposited, blinking, in the sunshine. Around the corner is the Octagon Tower and below it a superb view of the waterworks – a semi-circular pool, the canal and the Banqueting House.

From Anne Boleyn's Seat, or Surprise View, you'll have a fine view upriver to Fountains Abbey – the jewel in the crown of Studley Royal. It is best seen in winter when the leaves on the trees do not obscure the view.

From here a beaten mud path takes you through the woods along the top of the hill and past the pillared Temple of Fame to Anne Boleyn's Seat or Surprise View. You reach it and there below you, through the trees, is Fountains Abbey itself. In summer the view is more obstructed than in autumn when the brilliant leaves are falling, or in winter when weak sunshine washes the branches of the bare trees.

The trees need thinning to improve the view, but The National Trust doubtless has this job on its list of priorities.

It's when you see a restoration project such as that being undertaken at Studley Royal that you appreciate the real value of The National Trust. It has taken a few knocks in recent years, but then when an organisation celebrates its centenary a carp here and there seems to be par for the course. Is it too autocratically run? Who selects the properties that are accepted? You've heard the criticisms.

But the sheer size of this project – which is just one of the hundreds that are funded by public subscription – must vindicate the Trust's work. Who else would oversee the restoration of the broken edges of the canalized river, or the maintenance of the wind-eroded pillars in Fountains Abbey, and make sure that paths were maintained and access made easy? Who else would develop a long-term plan of woodland management to ensure that the estate remains healthy and its attractions in good shape for the generations that come after ours? The Government? Local councils? Both are subject to political whim and changeable economy. The Trust, I reckon, is the safest guardian, and from this high vantage point they can see exactly what needs doing to the woodland at Studley Royal.

Now the path drops down to the massive Half Moon Pond and it is time to follow its curve and go in search of Fountains Abbey. It's a warm day. Visitors sit on the white benches that are placed on the path around this scimitar-shaped lake. Pheasants peck at the long grass beneath the trees that rise up at either side of the River Skell, which flows into the lake at the top end. Finally, the Abbey hoves into view, its pink sandstone blushing in the afternoon sun.

You'll walk beside the river towards the Abbey, discovering that the riverbank here is a botanic garden in itself. Upon its steeply sloping banks grow bistort and lady's mantle, red campion and butterbur, meadowsweet and purple comfrey, Queen Anne's lace and buttercups, and from the slow-moving beer-coloured water emerges the white-flowered water hawthorn. Mimulus, the monkey flower, has found a foothold among the boulders at the water's edge. Trout pop up for midges and a moorhen steers her two chicks across to the opposite bank.

And finally you're there. Fountains Abbey has been described as 'the noblest

Studley Royal is not a garden with flowers, but its trees are stately specimens that give additional glory when reflected in the water. The effect is especially striking in autumn when fiery tints turn the water to amber or crimson.

monastic ruin in Christendom'. Walk around it and you will find it hard to disagree. It was founded in 1132 by a group of Benedictine monks who broke away from St Mary's Abbey in York and by 1135 it had been admitted to the Cistercian Order. The monks built their abbey from stone quarried from the side of the valley, and the River Skell provided them with water. Livestock thrived in the sheltered valley and the order prospered, except for a spell in the fourteenth century when the Black Death, Scots raids and bad harvests led to economic collapse. But the community recovered and prosperity returned under the abbacy of Marmaduke Huby at the turn of the fifteenth and sixteenth centuries. He built the great Perpendicular tower which symbolized his hope for the Abbey's future. The end of Fountains Abbey came in 1539 with the Dissolution of the Monasteries, when Henry VIII wreaked revenge on the Papacy for its failure to annul his marriage to Catherine of Aragon in order that he could marry Anne Boleyn.

The ruins are breathtaking in scale and especially fascinating – some parts are still astonishingly well preserved. There are vast arches and stairways made of stone that may be pink or purple, cream or ochre. The lay brothers' refectory is remarkably intact with a long and vaulted ceiling of amazing construction, and the tower still presides over all beneath it. Swallows keel through the lofty windowless arches in summer and in winter the wind whistles among the eight-hundred-year-old pillars.

A little further up the valley, past the museum, is Fountains Hall, built between 1598 and 1604 by Stephen Proctor. Some of the stone for the Hall came from the Abbey ruins. It's an imposing looking house, thought to have been designed by Robert Smythson, the Elizabethan architect of Hardwick Hall.

In front of it are plump cushions of clipped yew, but there is no garden, just

two squares of grass below its striking facade of storey upon storey of buff-grey stone, enlivened with leaded lights in mullioned windows.

The fact that John Aislabie's son, William, purchased the Abbey and the Hall has given Studley Royal a grand finale that is impossible to beat. Weary, but hugely impressed, you can wend your way up towards the brand new visitors centre taking the path at the side of Fountains Hall, and buy a postcard, take the weight off your feet, slake your thirst, satisfy your

The climb to the Octagon Tower is not for the squeamish – it's steep and there's a long, dark tunnel to be traversed. But the journey is well worthwhile. From its lofty eminence the views of the Water Garden below are spectacular.

hunger and reflect on the pleasures of the day. It will take you at least two hours to do the walk if you are to savour its delights to the full, and then you can walk, once more, down the riverbank to the car park beside the lake. Make a day of it with a picnic – you'll never forget it.

HIDCOTE MANOR

Gloucestershire

Up and down the country lanes of Warwickshire and Worcestershire, through the steeply rolling farmland at the heart of Britain, you will journey to find what is thought by many to be the most English of gardens, which is why it comes as a surprise to discover that the garden at Hidcote was made by an American. Well, he was born in America at any rate, even if he did come here at a rather young age. The garden certainly surrounds the kind of Cotswold manor house most Americans would do anything to get their hands on.

The man who made it was Lawrence Waterbury Johnston. His wealthy American mother, Gertrude Winthrop (she had remarried and been widowed again since the birth of her son), bought the house in 1907. Major Lawrence Johnston spent forty years creating this masterpiece before passing it on to The National Trust and moving to his other house in the French Riviera. He died there ten years later, doubtless dreaming about his English garden as he gazed with rheumy eyes over the blue Mediterranean.

OPPOSITE *The richly planted Red Borders at Hidcote Manor are terminated by twin gazebos. Behind them appear avenues of pleached hornbeams on stilts, leading the eye through wrought-iron gates to reveal a spectacular view of the Cotswolds.*

A view through one garden gives glimpses of those that lie beyond. From the Bathing Pool Garden, and the boy with the dolphin, you can see the fat topiary peacocks of the White Garden. The plants here provide a pallid show of flowers and a richness of scent.

It was the first property acquired by The National Trust specifically on account of its garden, and there is some amusing correspondence concerning its hand-over reprinted in the excellent guidebook.

At that time The National Trust was a possessor of land rather than property. It owned only six country houses, so

the prospect of inheriting a garden must have been daunting, but not nearly so daunting as the characters involved in the hand-over. Johnston, by this time, was old and crotchety, and the Trust's historic buildings secretary, James Lees-Milne, was, by all accounts, a man of forthright opinions. He noted in his diary that Johnston was 'a dull little man... Mother-ridden'. Well, maybe he was, but I rather admire Johnston who seems to me to have been more of his own man than he is given credit for.

He was educated in Britain in the 1890s, went to Cambridge to study for a history degree, became a naturalised British citizen, went off to fight in the Boer War, and then the First World War, eventually becoming a major. He left almost no documentation behind him about the creation of the garden at Hidcote, and had little to do with the Royal Horticultural Society. It strikes me that he was happiest doing his own thing. Good for him.

He cuts a mild figure in the photographs that I have seen. The classic old military buffer with a semi-walrus moustache and half-lidded eyes; fond of jodhpurs, tweed jackets, springer spaniels and dachshunds. In short, he seems to me to have a lot in common with PG Wodehouse's Lord Emsworth.

His mother, on the other hand, looks a frightful little woman. Bird-like and with a down-turned mouth, she glowers from her photograph. It is easy to believe that she was domineering. When she died she left her son only the interest from her considerable estate. That must have been hard for Johnston to swallow and was also the reason why, when he left Hidcote to The National Trust, he could not provide an endowment for its upkeep. But the Trust did take it on, and soon became gardeners as well as custodians.

In the Pillar Garden neat columns of clipped yew rise up from a thick underplanting of shrubs and border perennials. Between the hard lines at Hidcote, the generous growth of plants softens the overall effect of the formality.

Hidcote is where The National Trust learned the techniques of restoration, conservation and management that were applied to other gardens that came into its possession later. It is also the garden that influenced Vita Sackville-West and Harold Nicolson, who went on to create their own masterpiece at Sissinghurst.

I first visited Hidcote more than ten years ago and loved it, but I was curious to see how it had fared since then. I much prefer just to turn up and quietly get on with visiting a garden, but I really did want the treat of seeing this one unencumbered by flocks of visitors, so I asked to visit on an August day when the place was closed.

This I do and take a friend with me, just for swank. We motor up the drive on a warm summer morning, Cotswold gravel crunching under the tyres. Sheepishly we walk past other visitors who had turned up expecting the garden to be opened every day at all hours.

Finding our way in was the first problem but then, as the guidebook says, 'there is no set route around Hidcote, which new visitors occasionally find disconcerting'. And if you visit on a day when the garden is closed there is no set route for entry either! We find our way in through the plant sales area – tastefully carpeted with buff Cotswold chippings and centred by a Hidcote blue gazebo with a bobble on the top – but please, if you do visit the gardens, do me a favour and don't use this route!

The blue paintwork, rather like that at Snowshill Manor, is one of Hidcote's

The ancient cedar tree grew at Hidcote Manor when Lawrence Johnston came here with his mother in 1903. Now it hovers on the edge of the White Garden like a benign spectre, offering welcome shade in the heat of the summer.

trademarks and is a refreshing change from white or dark green. A cloister of oak and stone stabling surrounds this posh market-place, and the café along one side has a thatched roof. Gardeners from abroad must think they have died and gone to heaven.

We peer round corners and eventually find our way in past upper-crust potting sheds and lead cisterns stuffed with purple heliotrope and grey helichrysum. Blue tubs overflow with fuchsias. The house itself is a sturdy Cotswold pile – honey-stoned and capped with finials – and beyond the house the garden begins to unfold.

It is a series of rooms – each one different in mood – and is planted up with skill and good taste. Near to the

house is the ancient cedar – one of the few remaining trees that were here when Johnston and his mother arrived – and the patchwork of gardens spreads outwards from it.

The largest of these is the Theatre Lawn, a great sweep of grass with a raised circular stage at the end reached by a flight of steps decorated by stone fruits in stone urns and surrounded by a hedge. The long grass auditorium is bordered by a yew hedge pierced by several doorways. There are inviting portals in hedges and walls at every turn in the garden and, for the greatest pleasure, just take whichever turning captures your fancy.

From the 'rear stalls' end of the theatre lawn you can enter the Old Garden and

Even the parts of the countryside outside the grounds at Hidcote seem to have been created with garden effects in mind. Lawrence Johnston used them to dramatic effect – guiding the eye towards such views with hedges and borders and framing them with arches and gates.

tread on its pathway of broken staddle-stones. Pass beds of cottage garden flowers – phlox and dahlias, Michaelmas daisies and tender salvias, jostling with hydrangeas in tubs – and you will approach the spreading boughs of the ancient cedar tree. The first of the autumn cyclamen push up in August through soil full of pine needles and spread with chicken wire to prevent squirrels and the like from digging up the succulent corms.

Suddenly, to your right, you will spy an enchanting view past the Circle Garden, the Red Borders and the Stilt Garden. Go if you feel the urge, but I would advise you to postpone the pleasure until you have enjoyed the White Garden to your left.

Here fat-breasted peacocks clipped out of box sit as brooding finials at the corners of box bolsters that edge the four beds, each of them stuffed with phlox and roses, galtonia, tobacco plants, artemisia and acanthus. And the scent! The wonderful aroma of fresh cherry pie. Or is it Play-doh? The bed beside us is planted up with purple heliotrope.

Hidcote Manor sits comfortably within the garden – its honey-coloured walls, stone roofs and handsome chimneys are imposing enough to live up to the standard of the cleverly crafted garden, but not strong enough to overpower it. Each complements the other perfectly.

You will see, on the other side of the handsome stone wall, some cottages, now lived in by gardeners and the farmer and his family, all part of this small community. You will come across the gardeners now and again, quietly pottering among the plants – fork or hoe in hand, bent double in the beds and borders. An irrigation system helps the lawns stay green in summer, but as yet the borders have no such provision and sprinklers have to be lugged around.

Leave the White Garden and see where your nose takes you. It may be to the Fuchsia Garden or to the Bathing Pool Garden, where a cherub holds on to a dolphin (or is it a banana?) in the middle of a circular pool. Leading off it is a tiny little courtyard with a tiled floor and a thatched and pillared summerhouse. Here there is a shady spot to rest on old oak pews before taking a cobbled path lined

Whenever you reach the terminus of an avenue or a feature at Hidcote it pays to look in another direction. At right angles to the gazebos you can see here, at the end of the Red Borders, this view down the Long Walk.

with hostas in pots past groves of lilac lacecap hydrangeas that positively zing in the sunshine.

The cobbles beneath you have been polished by generations of feet and will lead you to a grassy circle that offers yet another quandary. Which exit shall we take? What will we find?

Tantalizing views open up every second or two, offering you just enough temptation to make the decision on which route to take incredibly difficult. Through the Hydrangea Garden and the Upper Stream Garden, where it is as informal as it gets, you will come to Mrs Winthrop's Garden. Now I do not wish to be further disparaging to the dear old mother of our hero, but her garden has recently been restored and the brick paviors are rather too new to fit in. The planting scheme is strident, too – yellow lysimachia and blue pansies, cabbage palms and a striped and spiky agave in a pot, hostas, euphorbias and blue petunias. The hedge surrounding this garden is of copper beech, decorated with a golden-leafed hop. Subtle it is not. No, I am not keen. We will move on.

Make your way up an *allée* of pleached limes towards the Red Borders, one of Hidcote's most dramatic features. These broad twin borders, either side of a central grass path, end in twin summerhouses, brick built with pointed roofs. The plants are fiery and dark bloomed in equal measure. There are crimson dahlias, red salvias and lobelia, purple buddleia awash with red admiral and tortoiseshell butter-flies. The deep plum foliage of Japanese maples and atriplex contrasts with orange daylilies and, as the summer matures, red rose hips decorate the arching branches of *Rosa moyesii*. Scarlet verbena and plum-leafed cannas, scarlet geraniums and begonias add to the heat and, eventually, it is a relief to escape up the stairs between the summerhouses into the Stilt Garden. Here pleached hornbeams stand on tall legs leading you to a pair of wrought-iron gates. And there it is – the most wonderful view over the undulating wheatfields of the Cotswolds: green pastures dotted with sheep and cattle and a vast acreage of sky.

Turn back when you have drunk your fill and retrace your steps to the summer-houses. Look through the doorway of the one on your right and you will see another tremendous view down over the Long Walk – a verdant strip that will inevitably lead your feet southwards to yet more views across ripening fields of corn, over which the swallows dart to catch their snacks of midges.

You will be tempted into the Pillar Garden – yew pillars with chunky square bases sculpted by shears. Here are lavender and agapanthus and Speciosum lilies – the overall effect is of blue, mixed with a little pink and yellow.

If the day is as baking as this one in August you will be glad to find seats tucked away in corners providing wonderful views. And there are embellish-ments to make you smile – watering-cans bolted to the bottom of a flight of garden steps; the portly peacocks in the White Garden, and the glimpses of that jolly blue paint.

So much is there to see that the tour can make you giddy, for when you have feasted your eyes on all the gardens on the south side of the house, there are yet more to the north – the Rose Borders and the Pine Garden with its inky-blue lily pool that is dive-bombed by dragonflies. The Kitchen Garden is now mainly devoted to raising plants for the rest of the garden, but there are still traces of the intensity of former cultivation – gnarled espalier apple trees and old greenhouses.

This is a garden to be visited during all seasons. There is much to learn about plant combinations, and so much to admire in terms of form and structure. Lawrence Johnston may well have been influenced by that great plantswoman Gertrude Jekyll, but then Johnston himself has probably influenced more gardeners than that bombazine-clad lady with the bun and the glasses.

Few people have found Hidcote a disappointment, and I know many who think of it as the best garden in Britain.

A visit to Hidcote during late June or early July will be perfectly timed as far as the shrub roses are concerned. There are great borders of them, and they also pop up in all the smaller gardens, offering not only a huge variety of flower colour but also fragrances that are matchless – especially on a warm summer's afternoon.

HINTON AMPNER

Hampshire

I SUPPOSE ONE GETS proprietorial about one's local stately home. Well, perhaps not proprietorial, but certainly it's easy to become partial to a place if the house is a beauty and the garden complements it well. If the bookstall and the tearoom are staffed by local villagers then there is even more reason to feel that the place is a part of your life. Such is the case with my own 'local', Hinton Ampner. It's only twenty minutes away by car and I go there occasionally to dream of what it must have been like to be lord of all you surveyed. To be Lord Sherborne, in fact. Ralph Dutton was the last of the line and he died in 1985, aged eighty-six. The state of the house and its contents, along with the dream of a garden, are really down to him. In the usual manner of a latter-day squire he seemed to devote his life to them.

Hinton Ampner is the name of the hamlet as well as the house itself which stands proudly, but not haughtily, on a ridge overlooking undulating Hampshire

OPPOSITE *The steps that lead down from Hinton Ampner are dotted with daisies and lady's mantle and overhung with roses. The house itself commands wonderful views over the Hampshire countryside. Once disfigured by Victorian extensions, the house was returned to its former Georgian glory by the last Lord Sherborne, Ralph Dutton, in the 1930s.*

Water lilies decorate the oblong pool that sits on the terrace outside the house. On a warm summer's day you will see dragonflies and damsel flies hovering over them.

countryside at Bramdean, near Alresford. On his death, Ralph Dutton bequeathed the entire estate, all 1,650 acres of it, to The National Trust. Become a member and you can be as proprietorial about this place as you like!

I'd visit Hinton Ampner if it had no garden at all – I'd go just for the views. From the village of Bramdean you turn off the road by the lodge through an imposing pillared and wrought-iron gateway, rumbling over a cattle-grid and snaking ever upward, past mature oaks and limes that cast their aged branches out across luxuriant pasture grazed by beefy cattle.

Even the car park gives you a taste of what's to come – an indication that no

detail, however small or apparently mundane, has been overlooked. It is of rolled pink hoggin and there are white lines painted upon it to make sure you park in an orderly fashion. Not bossy, just thoughtful. Not tarmac, but hoggin. Material of the countryside, not the town.

This is gracious living – even the ticket hut at the entrance is porticoed – and the drive sweeps round to the front of the house with its white-pillared Georgian entrance. Now I'm especially susceptible to Georgian houses, and that's what Hinton Ampner is, or rather was, and is again. I'll explain. The existing house is to the south of the original Tudor house which was demolished in 1793 'having been rendered uninhabitable by ghostly manifestations'. The Georgian house that replaced it was much altered in 1867 when such architecture was well out of fashion, and was encased in a kind of Victorian Tudor shell. Ralph Dutton (who lived in the house all his life but didn't become Lord Sherborne until his cousin died in 1982) restored the Georgian aspect of the house between 1936 and 1939, getting rid of the grisly Victorian cosmetic surgery.

He started work on the garden rather earlier than this, while his father was still alive and, with the help of two venerable head gardeners, he created a garden that perfectly fits the countryside over which

Views are especially cherished at Hinton Ampner. Here the lower branches of large trees are carefully pruned so that the statue at the end of the vista is perfectly framed.

The Temple. In photographs it appears much larger than it really is, rather like Queen Mary's Doll's House, but it is delightfully elegant and commands views down a tree-lined avenue and across rolling fields to the woodland opposite.

it presides; a garden for which Kipling's poem could have been written:

> *Our England is a garden that is full of stately views,*
> *Of borders, beds and shrubberies, of lawns and avenues*

In the valley below the south front of the house rises the River Itchen. All around are rolling fields of pasture and wheat, with the distant gamboge stains of oil-seed rape. Erupting regularly among the agriculture are mature copses of oak, lime and beech.

In *The Englishman's Garden*, published in 1982, Ralph Dutton remarks that it was the words of Alexander Pope, rather than Kipling, that he constantly bore in mind during the making of the garden here:

> *Let not each beauty ev'ry where be spy'd*
> *Where half the skill is decently to hide;*
> *He gains all points, who pleasingly confounds,*
> *Surprizes, varies, and conceals the Bounds.*

Ralph Dutton does, indeed, constantly surprise you as a visitor and allows the bounds of his garden to smudge themselves into the countryside.

Just before you reach the house, crunching your way up the drive, you'll come to a gate in a ten-foot-high wall on your right. Peep through the wrought iron,

decorated with its red and white quartered shields (though doubtless they are called something else in heraldry) and you will see the old Kitchen Garden. 'Private' says the sign, but you can still look down the central pathway and see old espalier apple trees to right and left and an urn at the end of the walk. The Kitchen Garden is an acre in size and completely walled, and even the least covetous of gardeners would kill for it. It's thought that the wall was built before the destruction of the Tudor house in 1793.

Then comes the quandary – where to go from here. The nice lady in the porti-coed bookshop sold me a handy plan and I decide to turn on my heels outside the Kitchen Garden gate and, with my back to it, head off between close-clipped box hedges which surround what the plan calls 'The Orchard'. The hedges quarter the ground which was once the site of the old Tudor house and the wizened apple trees that remain, barely half a dozen of them, are skirted with Queen Anne's lace, daffodils and wild flowers. At the corners of the four boxed enclosures are cones of close-clipped yew and directly ahead of you is an arbour, behind which Hinton Ampner church squats low, with its knapped flint walls and tiny tower with wooden shutters.

But another path beckons me down to the Magnolia Garden, a grassy ride that winds between the only lime-free borders in the garden. Here are the magnolias you would expect, with their waxy cups held up to the sky and azaleas and rhododendrons pushing up through a carpet of candelabra primulas. There are camellias, pieris and other lime haters, all leading you onwards. The path terminates at an urn set above a ha-ha with views of the farmland beyond. The lime haters here do not have the luxuriant feel of those in gardens on proper acid soil and, in some ways, this is the least exciting part of the garden. But, gardening on chalk myself, I can understand why Ralph Dutton wanted to broaden his range of plants and have a go.

I retrace my steps back towards the Church of All Saints, which contains a memorial tablet to Ralph Dutton, engraved with the wistful sentiment: 'The last of his line', and turn down another inviting pathway opposite the church gate, canopied by ash and evergreen oak, tulip trees and other exotics, underplanted with hardy geraniums and shade lovers. 'Dell View Path' the plan calls it, so I should have realised what was in store. The path skirts the eastern part of the garden, affording more fine views over the farmland and then suddenly down to the right you can see the Dell itself – a steep-sided chalk pit on whose sides are planted all manner of trees and shrubs. It's like looking down into a floral cauldron. A pink-blossomed

cherry hangs over a white-painted seat, behind which a massive purple-leafed rhubarb explodes from the soil.

Ralph Dutton reclaimed this area before the war, from the rubbish tip it had become, and planted it up with chalk lovers he had noted growing well in Sir Frederick Stern's chalk pit garden at Highdown in Sussex. But I am afraid he had not calculated for the difference in micro-climate – Stern's garden had freely-draining mobile air; the chalk pit at Hinton Ampner was a very effective frost pocket – and most of the plants failed to survive their first winter.

The war intervened and the pit was left to nature, finally to be reclaimed once

The main task in this garden over the past few years has been to reinvigorate shrubs and plants that have outgrown themselves. With careful pruning and feeding this is being achieved and a garden that was beginning to look old and tired is taking on a new lease of life.

more when hostilities ceased and turned into the sunken oasis that it is today.

When you've snaked your way right round and down the Dell View Path, you'll find yourself in the Dell itself. Look to the left up the Philadelphus Walk, a gently curving alleyway flanked by head-high box hedging lined with mock oranges and other shrubs that scent the air on early summer evenings.

You see, this is the problem at Hinton Ampner, you never quite know which way to turn. The Philadelphus Walk curves its way uphill; I walk downhill toward another quandary – another crossroads, with another farmland view to the left, a tremendous view to the right up across the terraces that run past the south side of the house, and a walk straight ahead that leads to the sunken flattened lawn that was once the tennis court.

I explore them all in turn, finding a couple with a baby gurgling its way across the flat-as-a-pancake tennis lawn, and

other folk sitting in the spring sunshine on benches that are dotted about the garden. Alongside most of the garden perimeter pathways are broad borders of shrubs fronted by aprons of hardy perennials. All along your route, flowers and plants are being offered for your delectation and inspection. It's clear that many of the shrubs are old and, in some cases, tired out, but it looks as if that's being remedied.

Anybody connected with Hinton Ampner will tell you that the new head gardener and administrator, Nick Brooks,

The topiary in the Sunken Garden is a Hinton Ampner trademark. Created just before the Second World War, these 'chessmen' sit above the Bastion, an apron of grass, which makes a stunning viewpoint across the valley.

and his staff of two have done amazing work over the last four years, replanting and rejuvenating beds and borders that have gone over the hill. I'd never met Nick Brooks so I asked the lady in the bookshop what he looked like, with a view to having a word. 'You can't miss him', she said. 'He has a long beard and a green jumper.' So far I have seen no sign of anyone remotely resembling a cross between WG Grace and Mr McGregor, only a handsome wooden wheelbarrow and a hoe parked by one of the borders at the front of the house indicate the presence of a gardener.

I move on, approaching the house along the route I have been saving until last – the broad south terrace which stretches way beyond the building itself to east and

west. The first enclosure is bounded by broad yew hedges with massive yew newel posts at the corners. In the centre is a wide urn planted up with sulphur-yellow wall-flowers on this May day, and around it are oblong beds of the same wallflowers inter-planted with white lily-flowered tulips.

Then it's up a wide flight of steps, past a long bed of 'Iceberg' roses and a canal-shaped lily pool to get your first proper look at the handsome Georgian house, with its rounded bay windows of mellow brick and its draperies of evergreen magnolia, *Abutilon vitifolium*, vines and solanum, and petticoats of finely-cut Japanese maples swishing out from the borders that abut the house.

And the view, oh, the view! Across the croquet lawn and the Sunken Garden

below dotted with the yew chessmen – the trademarks of Hinton Ampner – is a semi-circular apron of grass jutting out above the field below. This is the Bastion and from here you can stand, as though on the prow of a ship, and gaze out over the landscape, appreciating the fact that, as your eyes scan the valley, you are at a height roughly equivalent to the hills you can see on the far horizon.

How anyone inside this house ever got any work done I fail to see, because looking through any window must have presented them with a view that took all of their attention. Outside, on the terraces, the problem is compounded as yet more tempting vistas draw you on. There is the Long Walk – fully two hundred yards of it – pillared with Irish yews and bordered by shrub roses on one side and flowering shrubs on the other, then the Sunken Garden and then the Temple – a classical summerhouse of modest proportions, much smaller than it appears in photographs, in which are four chairs fitted with cushions. There is no one else in sight on this spring afternoon. I flop down on a chair to admire the view down the valley which leads the eye to an obelisk, sited at the end of an irregular avenue of venerable lime trees. A tortoiseshell cat rubs up against my leg, purring all the time.

What a way to spend an afternoon.

Tea. A cup of tea. At the end of the house is the tearoom, and in the tearoom is Jenifer – tall with grey hair and glasses and an apron that means business. I see her in church on a Sunday but was not aware that she worked here.

'Fancy you not knowing!', she says, as she passes a tray containing a teapot, a hot water jug, a cup and saucer and a plateful of cake to a man wearing a green jumper and a long beard. Nick Brooks has left his wheelbarrow to have his tea. I have my tea and cake with him and discover that he has been here four years, that the previous garden he looked after was in Montrose,

Scotland (far milder by the salt-water estuary), and that his biggest problem at Hinton Ampner has been the advanced age of many of the shrubs. They have needed dramatic pruning to re-invest them with the vigour they once had, and to achieve the effect that was originally desired.

'Informality is great,' he says, 'but a plant growing the way it wants to doesn't create that, it just creates a mess, so you've got to picture it and force it to do what you want it to do.'

But Nick Brooks admits the design of the garden at Hinton Ampner is 'fantastic', and describes it as a 'twentieth-century quest for tranquillity'. Ralph Dutton started work on the parkland, planted out the trees to make the views, then came into the garden and finally adjusted the house to make the most of the landscape he had created.

But where, I wanted to know, was the very best view? 'Ah, you won't be able to see that', he said. 'It was from his own private bathroom. There's a loo with a

It's not only trees and shrubs that fill up the beds and borders here. Mixtures of annuals and border perennials give pleasure, too. Here Eryngium giganteum, *otherwise known as Miss Willmott's ghost, shoots up through a carpet of pink-flowered diascias.*

view – it's in a little alcove with a small window that looks right out over the south park-land. He could have seen everything his gardeners were doing while he sat there and read his newspaper!'

The tea is finished and I decline another pot. The ginger cake (made by Nick's wife) was delicious (though I notice that he had a slice of sponge). Nick returns to his hoe and his wheelbarrow and I return home, wondering if I will ever be a Lord of the Manor in the style of Ralph Dutton. I'd rather like to be. There are few better memorials to leave behind you than a house and garden of the quality of Hinton Ampner. If Ralph Dutton's quest really was for twentieth-century tranquillity, then he achieved it quite perfectly. ❧

TREBAH

Cornwall

'THIS IS NO pampered, pristine, prissy garden with rows of clipped hedges, close-mown striped lawns and daily raked paths. You are going to see a magnificent old, wild and magical Cornish garden' – so says the leaflet written by Tony Hibbert who, with his wife Eira, now looks after Trebah's twenty-five-acre ravine that slopes steeply down to the Helford River.

From the top of the hill, on the road from Truro, you will see a snatch of the Falmouth estuary below, before circum-navigating a roundabout covered in moon daisies and following the signs to the quaintly named Mawnan Smith, and then onwards to the exotic-sounding Trebah.

Recorded in the Domesday Book as being the property of the Bishop of Exeter, Trebah passed through many Cornish owners before becoming the property of a Quaker family, the Foxes, who created a number of fine Cornish gardens, including Glendurgan right next door.

It was Charles Fox who planted the ravine in the 1840s – instructing his gardeners through a megaphone from the top windows of his house. The trees he positioned on the sides of the ravine form the backbone of today's planting.

OPPOSITE *If you look down the ravine at Trebah, past cabbage palms and tree ferns, the view is spectacular.*

The Hibberts acquired the property in 1980, but it wasn't until ten years later that they formed the Trebah Trust and so assured the garden's future. Visiting it today is a real adventure.

Now I sometimes hear warning bells when I read that a garden is 'magnificent, old and wild'. All too often these are just euphemisms for lack of tender loving care. Not so at Trebah. The whole feeling is most certainly 'shaggy' – film director Derek Jarman's greatest compliment to a garden – and there are areas that are undoubtedly wild, but this rugged ravine is sheltered enough to grow a wide range of plants that would be tender in most other parts of the country and you can't but marvel at their vigour and the fact that they make you feel about a foot tall.

The entrance to the garden is decidedly exotic. You walk down a narrow gravel path flanked by cordylines, Chusan palms (*Trachycarpus fortunei*), echiums, osteospermums, phormiums and diascias spilling over the tops of stone retaining walls, then into a plant centre where you buy your ticket and a host of tender plants for the garden, greenhouse, conservatory and windowsill – everything from rhodo-dendrons and tree ferns to bougainvilleas and bananas.

It's only a little niggle, but I wanted to go straight into the garden at this point,

Monstrous foliage abounds – you can walk beneath the leaves of the gunnera in Gunnera Passage. Elsewhere this gigantic rhubarb contrasts with finer fern fronds.

rather than be waylaid among the rustic poles and picnic tables. The first sign I saw said 'Tarzan's Camp' and my heart sank. Was this to be a garden designed for tourists, with vivid signs at every turn and rope ladders slung up every tree? I needn't have worried. Yes; there are ropes slung from a number of trees in 'Tarzan's Camp', alongside an aerial ropeway, but these are tucked away in a corner and the tree trunks from which they hang are so vast that you really could expect to see Johnny Weissmuller hurtling into view. It makes you smile rather than grimace.

From here the ground falls away down the valley. Soon you are so completely fazed by the size and number of plants that you forget about Tarzan and Jane and wonder at the richness of the planting and the paucity of your vocabulary. 'Gosh' was the word that kept coming to my lips.

The plan of the garden suggests several routes down the ravine and a few detours, too. I set off on a warm June day, feeling as if I were going on safari in the tropics.

In front of the house (which commands a view to die for) is an apron of lawn and, below it, right down the 'V'-shaped valley to the Helford River, an amazing mixture of rhododendrons and tree ferns, palm trees and gunneras – as though someone had taken all the exotic-looking plants on earth and sprinkled them generously on the slopes of the ravine. The temptation to explore is overwhelming.

From the apron of grass in front of the house there are wonderful views over the treetops to the Helford River.

I head up around the house first, toward the Koi Pool underneath overhanging New Zealand flax and hydrangeas on the narrow, light grey gravelled path which jinks this way and that, past boulders and mounds of foliage and flowers. There are places to sit on benches beneath palm trees and maples, tree heathers and camellias. The Koi Pool, when you reach it, is not large, but it is a cool spot with a tinkling waterfall tumbling over rocks behind it, and tree ferns springing up from the moist and shaded earth. The lurid fish with their blotches of orange and buff, blue-grey and salmon pink, twist and turn in the depths. Echiums and bright-flowered lampranthus spring out of cracks in the stone retaining walls that hold up the banks of the pool.

The thing to do now is to follow the water downhill – on its way to the Helford River with a spectacular journey in store. The Water Garden consists of the boggy margins of this stream, which just below the Koi Pool passes the widest swathe of arum lilies I've ever seen. This is the start of the grandeur of Trebah – the sheer richness of its plantings. The white upturned flowers – like a thousand

hunting horns turned upwards to the sky – push up among glossy green leaves for yard after yard, and then yellow Candelabra primulas appear to the right of the path to draw your attention away from the lilies. It is as if all the plants in this garden are competing with one another for your attention – 'me, me, me!', they cry – like schoolchildren showing off to Miss.

Now there are tree ferns to turn you green with envy. Their fibrous trunks rise ten feet or more into the air, to be topped with a parasol of finely cut fronds. There are no signs saying 'Don't touch' and it is good to be able to feel the coarse texture of the trunks and gently to caress the tips of the fronds that are within reach.

More paths take off to left and right to confuse you, through foxgloves and bracken, a truly wild patch, through The Bamboozle with its thicket of bamboos. I'm trying to stick to the track called The Beach Path which leads right down to the river. But how do I resist the temptations along the way?

Dinky's Puddle is a patch of mud in which grow monkey flowers and skunk cabbage, while at Peter's Bridge is a sight that stops me in my tracks. The Pocket handkerchief tree, *Davidia involucrata*, is in full bloom. This massive tree, rounded in shape, has white pocket-handkerchief flowers hanging from its spreading branches. Its other names are the dove tree and the ghost tree – a sign below it, knocked into the soil, shows a white-sheeted ghost. This is just one of a number of signs that I've noticed near prominent trees and shrubs. A look at the guide tells me that these are all part of the 'Trebah Trail' for children.

Now plants are often a problem for children. Animals are easy; they are cuddly and they do things. Few plants are cuddly, and they don't move very fast. Like the cows in PG Wodehouse's *Blandings Castle*, they 'lack sustained dramatic interest.' As a result it is tricky to get most children

The path through the Water Garden will take you past moisture-loving irises and arum lilies – a view that changes with the seasons.

Tree ferns grow well at Trebah. Here they are underplanted with brilliant candelabra primulas – both enjoying the moist soil.

interested in gardening – the seeds just don't grow fast enough. What children need is the 'gosh' factor and features like the Gunnera Passage provide it.

Now I've seen the prickly rhubarb, *Gunnera manicata*, in a number of settings over the years, but I've never seen it grow to such a size or planted in such large numbers. The passage runs from one side of the ravine bottom to the other and walking beneath these green parasols is rather like walking under a forest of umbrellas on a rainy day at the Chelsea Flower Show. It's sensational – the spiky leaf stalks are ten feet tall and the leaves six

feet across. Children rave over it (or under it) and so do grown-ups.

Walk to and fro until you can take no more and then wander further down the valley, which is now completely planted from side to side with hydrangeas. There are three acres of them – their flowerheads a profusion of azure mops.

Look back up the valley now and you'll see the white-painted house sitting at the top, master of all it surveys. It is just a short walk from here down to the Mallard Pond, with the breeze rippling its surface to silver and coots honking among the reeds, and then, from over the wall, you'll hear the tell-tale sound of the waves – the Helford River. Well, it's the sea really. The surf is crashing on to the sandy beach, where a few visitors to the garden have put down

their towels and are watching the sailboats out on the water.

This is Polgwiddon Cove, also known as Yankee Beach. A memorial stone sunk into the garden within earshot of the waves tells you why: 'To the officers and men of US 29 Infantry Division who embarked from Trebah in June 1944 for the D-Day assault on Omaha Beach, Normandy. We will remember them.'

Breathe in the sea air for as long as you like, then make your way back up by another path and mop up the bits you've missed. When you reach the top of the ravine, plonk yourself down on one of the seats and take in the view again, or go and search the garden centre for things you've seen and can't possibly do without. Then you can get in your car and say 'gosh', reminding yourself that you've really been in Cornwall and not Madeira.

HAMPTON COURT PALACE

Surrey

BUCKINGHAM PALACE HAS nothing on Hampton Court: it is dull and grey and it squats like an old broody hen at the end of The Mall. Hampton Court Palace, on the other hand, has all the attributes a good palace should have: it is majestic, it is big, it is built of the most wondrously warm brick, it vibrates with colourful history and it is, above all, friendly. It is also one of those palaces where the monarch seems to have stepped outside just for a moment, and you can expect his return at any time.

The monarch in question is Henry VIII, for although Hampton Court Palace was built by Cardinal Wolsey, it was actually commandeered by Henry VIII when Wolsey fell from grace in 1528. And yet as far as the gardens go, it is a later monarch – William III – whose influence is now in greater evidence than any other, thanks to the most exciting historic gardening project undertaken in Britain this century: the restoration of the Privy Garden.

OPPOSITE *Until recently an overgrown shrubbery, King William III's Privy Garden at Hampton Court has now been restored to its former intricate glory.*

I can never stop myself from feeling a surge of excitement when I visit Hampton Court. The atmosphere positively crackles, and amid the convoluted shapes of warm, mellow brick, Henry VIII's Great Hall rises up majestically. The Tudor part of the Palace is fascinating and the King's apartments, built behind a Baroque facade by Sir Christopher Wren for William III, are out of this world – the glossy guidebooks will make you gasp: everywhere gilt and swags of red velvet can be found and there are priceless old masters and exquisite furniture. But, because of the title of this book, I must stay outside!

Until now, you could argue that the gardens of Hampton Court do not quite measure up to the Palace. But take a look inside the Palace in Leonard Knyff's painting of 1703; it shows Hampton Court Palace and its surrounding gardens and you will see that very little remains of the original elaborate layout. Along with Blenheim it was the nearest thing we had to Versailles, and William III considered Louis XIV his great rival.

So what is there to see today? Quite a bit. You will enter the Palace grounds from the A308 – whether you arrive from

the direction of Kingston upon Thames, Thames Ditton or Sunbury, and you will find yourself looking at the Tudor Palace full in the face. This is good on two counts: first, because you will see the Palace in historic order – the Tudor part

To the east front of Hampton Court Palace lies the Great Fountain Garden which was an elaborate parterre until Queen Anne brought about its demise. Clipped umbrellas of yew and formal beds now provide the ornamentation.

first and the eighteenth-century additions later, but also because the best part of the garden will be left till last.

Park your car in one of the many surrounding car parks and walk towards the West Front of the Palace. Turn left, and then on your left you will come to the Rose Garden, a formally laid out series of flower-beds, where anachronistic hybrid teas and floribundas delight the locals who, like everyone else, can get into the gardens free of charge – it is only the palace apartments for which a fee is exacted.

The Rose Garden and the adjacent gardens and tennis courts are all built within the tall brick walls that enclosed Henry VIII's Tiltyard – a place for sporting activities from archery to jousting. You can wander from one area to another,

discovering trees among grass, awash with daffodils and narcissi in spring, and borders against walls that are still planted up with traditional 'Parks Department' bedding in May and June for a summer of brilliance.

Then, as you start to circumnavigate the Palace, you will enter the Wilderness. Cardinal Wolsey enclosed it as part of his parkland and Henry VIII had his Great Orchard here, filled with all manner of fruit trees as well as oaks, elms and hollies – in those days it wasn't just fruiting trees that went into an orchard.

It was William and Mary who created the Wilderness which, at that time, was not just an overgrown wild garden but 'a place in which to walk along hedge-lined pathways laid out in a geometric design'.

Little of the geometric design remains today, except for the famous maze.

The maze is a 'puzzle maze' planted up in the 1690s by William's gardeners. At that time it was made mainly of hornbeam but it is now composed largely of yew. I don't know why, but it's never impressed me that much, even though the account in Jerome K Jerome's *Three Men In A Boat* of Harris trying to get into it and out of it is quite a giggle. 'Harris said he thought it was a very fine maze, so far as he was a judge.' Good

Part of the Pond Yard, a series of formal gardens occupying the ground where Henry VIII kept fish to supply the royal kitchens. The gardens are surrounded by hedges on stilts, and elaborate chimneys decorate the rooftop above the Tudor palace.

for Harris. I'm just impatient to get to the other side of the Palace.

You see, with the delights of the maze and the Tiltyard behind you, you're on your way to greater things. You'll go through a tall brick wall, turn to the right and suddenly find yourself walking along Sir Christopher Wren's baroque east front.

This is the Broad Walk, and looking out from the building across the park you'll appreciate the grandeur of the Great Fountain Garden – twenty-five acres laid out in a vast semi-circle with an avenue of lime trees, the originals of which were planted by Charles II.

In Henry's time the Broad Walk was a moat, but now it has been filled in and its liquid glory replaced by the Long Water – a canal which runs in a straight line beyond the huge semi-circle. Within the semi-circle are vast umbrellas of yew, clipped flat at head height and then domed at the top. Underneath them, on the wide hoggin driveways outside the east front, are carriages with liveried grooms waiting to take you on tours of the grounds. Beneath the trees is smoothly-mown grass which, in summer, becomes the venue for the Hampton Court Music Festival, where world famous tenors produce their top Cs in front of audiences parading the lawns and sheltering under corporate marquees. The marquees were there the last time I visited; empty and silent, waiting for their evening of operatic glory. Hefty lights were grouped under the yew trees, ready to illuminate the east front once darkness fell.

At the foot of the tall brick walls at either side of this facade are herbaceous borders, beefed up with annuals in summer. Look at them, and then look out beneath the umbrellas of yew and imagine what it would be like if this garden were to be returned to its former glory – the way William and Mary had it. You can see it on Knyff's painting when it was the Great Parterre, designed in the Dutch style by

Frenchman Daniel Marot who was famous for his decoration of Delft vases. There were thirteen fountains in this garden and elaborate patterns of box scrolls and gravel. Hollies and yews were clipped into obelisks, and some of the 'umbrellas' that are here now are the remnants of that earlier formality.

On William's death his sister-in-law, Queen Anne, considered the upkeep of the parterre too great an expense. Neither did she like the smell of box. But then, Queen Anne is famous for her legs rather than her green fingers. It was dug up and all the fountains, except the central one, were filled in. A semi-circular canal was dug on the outer limits of the parterre, lawns were laid and paths were re-aligned. It was known as the 'English Style', and it remained little changed throughout the Georgian period, which is something of a surprise considering that in 1764 'Capability' Brown was appointed head gardener at Hampton Court. It was Brown who created the natural look and who swept away formality. But even he was intimidated by Hampton Court and

The grand entrance to the park from the Great Fountain Garden. The bridge crosses over the Canal which feeds into the Long Water.

claimed that he had not destroyed its symmetry 'out of respect to himself and his profession', though he did allow the yews and the hollies to grow naturally. It was not until 1919 that the yews were clipped again, and many that had been felled fifty years earlier were replaced. The Lime Avenue that borders the Long Water was replanted in 1987 and, in recent years, this part of the grounds has become home to the hugely successful Hampton Court Flower Show. This takes place in July and is a summer version of the Chelsea Flower Show. Will the Great Parterre ever be seen again? There is a faint glimmer of optimism, on account of what has happened just around the corner.

Outside the windows of the east front of the Palace in summer are the citrus fruits that have been removed from the Orangery behind them. They stand in massive white half barrels, coopered with dark green bands, flaunting their fruits in

The Rose Garden is filled with a collection of modern hybrid teas and floribundas set in formal beds among the green lawns. This part of the garden was Henry VIII's Tiltyard where all manner of sporting activities took place, including jousting.

the morning sun. Walk past them and turn right at the end of the east front through the gateway in the wall and you will see a most remarkable sight: the newly restored Privy Garden, laid out exactly as it was for William III.

On my previous visit to Hampton Court the Privy Garden was an overgrown mixture of yews and hollies and shrubs. Some of them dated from the original Privy garden, but were no longer in any way formal. At the end are the famous Tijou Screens: elaborate wrought-iron works of art built by Jean Tijou who had his workshop on Hampton Green. You had to go on safari to find them before the restoration, now they are in full view, just as they would have been nearly three hundred years ago.

Garden historians will quiver with delight; folk with little back gardens will simply say 'gosh', but nobody can fail to be

impressed by the work which has brought this elaborate garden back to life. There are raised grassy banks at either side – that to the right is bounded by a huge arched pergola, Queen Mary's Bower, made of oak over which will be trained pleached hornbeams, and below is the intricately patterned garden with scrolls of dwarf clipped box enclosing areas of gravel, flower-beds or '*plattes bandes*' and pyramids of yew and holly. Thanks to an abundance of documentary evidence, plans and architectural remains, it has been possible to reconstruct the garden with great accuracy, even down to the flowering plants that were used within it (the schemes were changed three times a year, in March, June and September). Even the statues have been put in their original places. It will be a treat to watch this garden develop, and the view from the apartments above is now sensational – as far as the Tijou Screens and the River Thames – when once it revealed only a boscage of dark evergreens.

Walk on, when you can tear yourself away, down the broad flagged path alongside the Palace, which has formal gardens both to left and right, and another

Said to be the oldest known grapevine in the world, the vine at Hampton Court was planted between 1768 and 1774 by Lancelot 'Capability' Brown. The grapes it produces are sold to the public in late summer and early autumn.

Hampton Court legend at the end. There is a little knot garden on your right, planted in 1924 with a view to showing what the garden was like in the reign of Elizabeth I. It is a tiny pattern of foot-high clipped box, infilled with the kind of dwarf Semperflorens begonias and antirrhinums that are decidedly Queen Elizabeth II.

Opposite is the Pond Garden. This is a sunken garden on three levels with a fountain at its centre and summer bedding of a brilliance that will make you reach for your Ray Bans. You look at it, as you look at the garden adjacent to it, over a low brick wall beneath a pleached screen of limes, dotted with beech and holly, into which large windows have been cut.

Behind you, now, is a long, low lawn running alongside part of the Tudor Palace, above which are towering and ornately-patterned brick chimneys, sitting like chessmen on the rooftops. The lawn is surrounded by borders in which grow roses and border perennials, including the tender spires of echiums, usually only hardy in the West Country but here sending up azure columns of bloom against the warm brickwork. There are palm trees, too – *Trachycarpus fortunei* – some twelve feet tall. Not something the Tudors would have grown.

This entire area is known as the Pond Yard or the Glass Case Garden – it is where Henry VIII had his pools to supply fish for the royal kitchens, and where William and Mary had the carpenter Henrick Floris build them a glass case to house some of the exotic plants they brought from Holland. William and Mary may well have had one of the earliest British greenhouses.

The only greenhouse here now is at the very end of this broad flagged path, and it houses the famous grapevine planted by 'Capability' Brown between 1768 and 1774, making it the world's oldest known grape-vine. Outside is a huge area of well-manured soil, looking as though it is waiting for vegetable seeds to be sown. But no; this is where the vine's roots grow, and it's kept clear and enriched just to allow the vine to carry on growing vigorously. And grow it does. I have heard tell that its roots go out into the River Thames on the other side of the garden wall. Is it true? I don't know, but it's a good story.

Inside the lean-to, white-painted greenhouse is a board that gives the history of the vine and its cropping abilities:

The vine is recorded to have produced 1,800 lbs of grapes in 1798 and 2,245 lbs in 1807. Today it crops between 500 and 700 lbs. The full crop of black eating grapes is sold to visitors in the Palace shops in late summer or early autumn.

The public were first allowed to see the vine in the 1840s when Queen Victoria opened the grounds to visitors. It might have been cropping rather more heavily then, but today it is still hugely impressive, filling the rafters with rods and leaves, through which the hundreds of bunches

of grapes dangle at the end of summer. You couldn't get your arms around the vast, knobbly trunk.

The vine is a kind of terminus for this series of gardens and when you reach it you might think that you have done the gardens at Hampton Court. Not quite. There is one more garden, redolent of the twentieth century, which many visitors miss, and that is the Apprentice Garden.

Retrace your steps along the east front, and then cut across the grass to the left of the Great Fountain, towards the left-hand end of the canal which runs around it. There you will pass down a snicket covered with greenery into a garden that was developed from the mid-seventies onwards by George Cooke, who was superintendent of the gardens from 1974 to 1990.

Here you would never guess you were in Hampton Court. There are trees and shrubs in great variety, a modern herb garden surrounded by trellis, a pool, a fruit and vegetable garden, and informal beds of perennials. There are trials of hedging plants, a pavement planted up with thymes and other carpeters, and an old hay rake which was used when this was a meadow.

It is not a great garden in its own right, but it is a wonderful sheltered haven which is sadly overlooked by many visitors who might appreciate a quiet sit down. They can do so on a seat placed here in memory of George Cooke, a man I knew when he was apprentice master of the Royal Parks and I held the position of supervisor of staff training at Kew.

George is one of the dozens of gardeners and monarchs who have left their mark at Hampton Court. Walk down the avenues and garden paths and you can feel their presence. Perhaps, once the Privy Garden is established in the affections of visitors, there might be a movement to recreate the Great Parterre and make Hampton Court a real competitor with Versailles. It is, after all, just what King William III wanted. Is it something King William V could achieve?

Aside from the sixty acres of gardens there is plenty of parkland to delight the visitor to Hampton Court. In spring the blossoming trees stand on a green carpet that is speckled with daffodils and narcissi, and in autumn the leaves on the trees turn fiery orange.

PACKWOOD HOUSE

Warwickshire

I AM NOT ONE of those who knocks the Midlands. I have worked there enough to know that it has areas of great beauty, from Stratford upon Avon to Wenlock Edge. But what I like about Packwood House is that you come across it unexpectedly in an area where it is, well, unexpected. It is barely eleven miles south-east of Birmingham, in the crook of the M42 and the M40 just a few miles from Solihull, and yet you seem to be in the heart of the country when you drive up to the house and its outbuildings of mellow, pale sienna-coloured brick.

There is more than a touch of Shakespeare about the place, mainly, I guess, because it is set in the Forest of Arden where, according to the Bard, Rosalind dressed as a feller in *As You Like It*. Not that the house looks terribly Shakespearean. It dates from the late sixteenth century, but those who came after made a few alterations to the original timber-framed house. It was later rebuilt

OPPOSITE *The view through the wrought-iron gates at Packwood to the green quadrangle is inviting – the wide herbaceous borders spill their plants on to the flagged path.*

in brick and is now rendered over in rather dull cement. But I don't want to do it a disservice. In spite of a costume that is rather drab for a Shakespearean character, it is a friendly house with a gem of a garden.

You'll get a sniff of it when you motor down the drive. Great columns of yew are pushing up over the hedge to your left like

The planting of beds and borders here is planned for continuous interest.

gigantic chessmen intent on escaping from their chequer-board.

Park by the stables and other warm, russety outbuildings and cross the lane to the entrance. You will enter a large grassy quadrangle through a delectable black-painted wrought-iron gate, and to right and left you will find deep herbaceous borders which today, in early June, are stuffed with hardy geraniums, catmint and bleeding heart.

The York stone path will lead you to the rear wing of the house which is used as the ticket office, and high up on the wall a blue-and-white painted sundial caressed by the rough leaves of a wall-trained fig tree will tell you how late it is.

It is time to get to the garden, through another black wrought-iron gate where bright yellow Welsh poppies push up between brickwork and bars. This is the Carolean Garden, walled on all four sides, with a brick-built gazebo at each corner. I would be happy to own just one of them, never mind four, but if I could pick just one it would be the one in the north-east corner – it's a real treat. Dating from the reign of Charles II it is square with a pyra-midal roof and a diamond pattern on its brickwork. Adjacent to it is a fireplace and a chimney, not for the comfort of visitors, but for the comfort of the peaches that grew against the wall that was heated by the flue.

The man responsible for handing over the house and garden to The National Trust was Graham Baron Ash. He did much to restore both of them to their former glory. The house was originally bought in 1905 by his father, Alfred, whose fortune had been made in the metal industry in Birmingham. He also owned racehorses and sounds a jovial sort of cove.

The remarkable Yew Garden is Packwood's most famous feature. Said to represent the Sermon on the Mount, some of these towering columns of clipped yew date from 1650.

'A big, rather swarthy man – with a mass of curly hair… He viewed life from the sunny side – and from the interior of a gorgeous Rolls Royce.'

Graham Baron Ash (known to his intimates as Baron) was sixteen when the house was bought, and he inherited it on his father's death in 1925. Father and son between them enlarged and restored the house, using what you might call architectural salvage for their improvements. Doors were bought from old houses, along with panelling, beams and so on. Much was bought from nearby Baddesley Clinton – a medieval moated manor house well worth a visit – when its owner fell on hard times. Great attention was paid to detail in Packwood's restoration, and on one occasion in 1938, when Baron Ash was

High Sheriff of Warwickshire, he is reported as having 'entertained on a dazzling scale'. Rather fittingly, there were open-air performances of Shakespeare.

To stay with Mr Ash in his house must have been something akin to staying with royalty. Listen to James Lees-Milne: 'He was invariably spruce, dressed in well-ironed lounge suits which betrayed that he was not really a countryman. He was infinitely correct, yet not stiff or stuffy. Anxious yet welcoming. A trifle over-sensitive yet infinitely kind. A very good host, he loved entertaining (his food was always delicious) so long as his guests did not stay too long and were at least half as tidy as himself. For he hated disorder.'

The ordered mind is something that is reflected in the garden, but not obsessively so. The lines are crisp and clean, the borders are laid out within hard formal lines, and the topiary, for which Packwood is famous, is sharply clipped. It has to be said that the standard of gardening at Packwood is remarkably high; the broad herbaceous border that runs along one wall of the Carolean Garden is as fine a blend of perennials as you will see anywhere in the country, and the Sunken Garden,

The cold plunge bath, dating from 1680, is not exactly inviting.

constructed by Baron Ash to replace flowerbeds that were grassed over during the war, has a central pool decorated with two lead putti arguing over a seashell.

But it is the twin herbaceous borders on the raised walk that runs above the Carolean Garden that I like best. Now, in early June, they are jam-packed with geraniums and centaureas, hostas and irises. Tradescantias add a splash of purple-blue, and towering kniphofias thrust their red-hot pokers of vermilion and yellow through masses of grassy foliage. These twin borders are set at either side of a York stone path that runs between two of the gazebos, and the view from one end to another is matchless.

And then you will see the gate that leads you into the Yew Garden. Go through it, making your way down the most delectable flight of semi-circular brick steps, but break off from your gasps at the sight of the tall columns of yew to look back at the wall behind you. There are thirty niches built into the brickwork – they are bee-boles – to house those rounded domes of straw called skeps that pre-dated beehives.

Then you can let yourself go and marvel at the yews – great fingers of green sticking up at the sky for thirty feet and more. Some of the yews are thought to have been planted by a previous owner of the house, John Fetherston, between 1650 and 1670. The Yew Garden is said to represent the Sermon on the Mount, but the row of tall yews known as the Apostles was not planted until the 1850s, so it is difficult to know whether this is what John Fetherston had in mind.

Whatever the true origins of the tableau of trees, the effect is amazing and dramatic. There are twelve towering Apostles, four monstrous Evangelists and one single yew tree, the Master, at the top of a huge mound of clipped box. This is a really neat trick – from below you don't see the spiral path that climbs the mound, just the occa-

The Sunken Garden encloses a rectangular pool. Flowering shrubs and carpeters overflow from the raised beds that surround it.

sional head bobbing among the greenery. This path winds on and on until eventually it reaches the top, from where there are stunning views down between the countless majestic pillars of yew – the Multitude – towards the house and garden, across a wild-flower-filled orchard and over towards the lake.

You can walk right round this, through a patch of woodland, and then return to take a look at the side of the house you have not yet seen.

There is a strange sunken area built of stone in a corner of this garden. The water dribbling into it is actually pumped from the lake. It is not particularly picturesque, but it is modestly surrounded by its own yew hedge. There is a reason for this; you are looking at a cold plunge bath dating from 1680.

Now I don't wish to cast aspersions on Mr Fetherston and his brood, who occupied Packwood House for 300 years,

but I do think they might have poured some of their efforts into seeking out a more comfortable mode of ablution. To come out into the centre of the Forest of Arden in the middle of the seventeenth century to have a dip in a cold pool of rather dubious water while being overlooked by half the cast of the Sermon on the Mount is not my idea of luxury.

Neither can I believe that Graham Baron Ash would ever have dipped his toe in the waters there. Unless, of course, that was what the reporter back in 1938 meant when he described the entertainment as being 'on a dazzling scale'.

Mind you, it's a phrase that is as applicable to the Yew Garden at Packwood today as ever it was to the High Sheriff's parties back in the thirties.

PARCEVALL HALL GARDENS

North Yorkshire

GARDENS ARE A bit like paintings – you can admire them in their setting, but you wouldn't necessarily want to take them home. There are thirty-one favourite gardens in this book. They are all special in one way or another, but if I had to choose the house and garden in which I could live, then it would be Parcevall Hall.

For a start it's in the Yorkshire Dale in which I was born and brought up – Wharfedale – the Queen of the Dales, soft-bosomed and welcoming, always. It nestles between Bolton Abbey and Burnsall, two places I love, and it is to be found at the end of a road that leads nowhere else which means it is quiet, well situated and blissful.

You can approach the village of Apple-treewick from several directions and all of them will give you a taste of Wharfedale. You can travel on the B6265 from Pateley Bridge, or on the B6160 from Burnsall or Bolton Abbey, but eventually you will be funnelled down a lane towards Appletree-wick and Parcevall Hall. I think that's the

OPPOSITE *The Rock Garden in Silver Wood at Parcevall Hall surrounds a pool that is backed by tall pyramids of* Picea glauca albertiana *'Conica'.*

spelling we've settled on. It's been Percival Hall, Parsable Hall, Persevells, Parse Hall and even Parson's Hall in the past.

It's a house with a history. It once sheltered the 'notorious local highwayman' Will Nevison, who made many a spectacular escape from the clutches of the excisemen. The present building dates from the sixteenth century, but the Manor of Appletreewick belonged to Bolton Priory before its dissolution in 1539, and fifty years after that 'Persevells' farm is recorded as having been left in the will of one Peter Yorke to his second son Thomas.

It's a lovely house of dull grey stone with mullioned windows, set on the south-facing slopes of the valley and commanding views to the rocky outcrops of Simon's Seat on the moors opposite. In winter this is a chilly place to be – the kitchen garden is a real frost pocket according to the head gardener – but in summer the three main terraces of this miniature Powis Castle garden are bathed in warm sunshine.

Not until 1927 did the gardens begin to take shape. It was then that the house was purchased by Sir William Milner, who chose the site because the ground was composed partly of limestone and partly of millstone grit.

He restored and enlarged the house, pulled down a barn, and began the construction of three major terraces on

Welsh poppies spring up among the water-worn limestone – home to a rich and varied selection of rock plants.

On one of the terraces a sculpture sits in the centre of a pool. It reflects Jesus's offer to the woman at the well in Samaria – water springing up to everlasting life.

the slope below the house. Navvies were recruited locally, the heavy hauling was done by horse and cart, and rock and stones were brought from the moors. Thirty men laboured over three years to make the garden in its present form.

Along with a succession of head gardeners and, at one time, thirteen under gardeners, Sir William continued the improvements, with a little help from friends like Lord Grey of Howick – a great rhododendron grower – and Mr Johnson of Caerhays in Cornwall. He was fortunate in obtaining plants that had been gathered by Reginald Farrer (another Yorkshireman who lived at Ingleborough Hall) and George Forrest who collected in China and Tibet. Some of these plants still survive. Queen Mary was Sir William's godmother and came to visit him at Parcevall Hall on several occasions.

Today the hall is used as a diocesan retreat, but the garden is still open to the public from spring to autumn. Whatever the season and whatever the weather it is always worth the journey.

I last visited on a warm June day: down the lanes, following the signs, with dry-stone walls to left and right; a weasel runs across the road and legs it up and over the limestone boulders. Round a corner I motor, past a cottage or two, and then cross a stream over a flat bridge with white-painted rails – the entrance to the drive of Parcevall Hall. The road rises now, and nips between the narrow alley that divides two gardener's cottages. Down to the left is a walled kitchen garden and then the steep lane passes St Cuthbert's Cottage – its narrow front borders awash with poppies and aquilegias – before coming to a full stop in a car park at the top of the hill.

There is no one about, just an honesty box in the wall, a few boxes of plants that are for sale, and half a dozen cars. The air is warm and a breeze rustles through the leaves of a nearby sycamore. There's a little hut at the entrance but no one is in it, so I make my way towards the garden, past a narrow border filled with peonies and delphiniums, Welsh poppies, cosmos and foxgloves – it's a border where spring and summer merge.

Little signposts put you in a quandary. Shall I go to the Orchard, or to Colin's Garden, or the Rock Garden, the Cliff Garden or the Terraces?

I wander through a patch of woodland which then deposits me by a pool, fed by a stream and surrounded by water-worn limestone. Suddenly I'm in a rocky woodland glade, where the low-sweeping branches of a full-skirted, cream-flowered *Viburnum plicatum* 'Mariesii' shine in the dappled shade. Here can be found serried ranks of candelabra primulas in glowing tones of orange, yellow and rose red. Vast rhododendrons tumble over the rocks alongside pyramids of *Picea glauca albertiana* 'Conica' that are a good ten feet high. This is the Rock Garden in Silver Wood where, surprisingly, some of the rhododendrons are established on limestone soil. It's delightfully wild and woolly, with carpets of sweet woodruff that are perforated by ferns and Solomon's seal.

Through the trees you can glimpse the tops of the moors on the other side of the valley, as you are tempted to walk down towards the house.

Past the house I walk, while the sound of monastic chanting drifts out of the windows, and only then do I see a sign saying that the top terrace is private.

A smart sidestep down a level enables me to look back at the house and its draperies of ceanothus and 'Albertine' roses, its shawls of wisteria and actinidia. There are sun-warmed beds of border perennials and mixed shrubs. Spiky spires of pink-flowered *Morina longifolia* push up in a colony and low domes of cistus, osteospermums and stachys make thick rugs.

On the next level down there are more mixed borders of roses and irises, shrubs and perennials and flat lawns that offer stupendous views of the moors beyond and of the softer sides of the valley. A pergola furnishes the end of this second terrace, and steps lead down in the centre to the next level, where a semi-circular pool

In spring daffodils carpet the floor of the orchard at Parcevall Hall.

nestles under the steps, and a rectangular water-lily pool draws your gaze on a warm afternoon. Clipped yew hedges act as dividing walls, and at the opposite end of the terrace from the pool is my second favourite seat – a west-facing wooden bench backed by honeysuckle and flanked by twin clumps of that deliciously fragrant daylily, *Hemerocallis lutea*. Its bright yellow blooms are held at eye and nose level. I sit for fully half an hour and can barely tear myself away, not only from the wonderful view across the valley, and the scent of the flowers, but also from the regular stream of visitors who marvel at the tall *Crinodendron hookerianum*, whose rose-red strawberry-shaped flowers dangle from its branches. Is it a fuchsia? How does it grow here in a garden that is so cold in winter? I know – I asked one of the gardeners. They cover it with old pea netting to keep off the frosts.

But now it's time to go in search of my favourite seat, and that is to be found in a wilder part of the garden – well, not really the garden at all, even though they call it

the Cliff Garden. To find it you must walk back through Silver Wood and the Rock Garden – which is no hardship at all – and then up through the Orchard – a lovely place with bench seats and tables among the rich carpets of wild flowers that stud the long grass under the spreading limbs of old apples and pears.

Then you'll see the sign to the Cliff Garden. It's a steep and narrow sheep track that takes you out of the main valley and up the side of a ravine that runs behind the house. On the sides of this deep gully, among the grass, are wild Farndale daffodils in spring, and now, in June, sheets of lavender-blue aquilegias and yellow Welsh poppy.

The view is breathtaking and at the top is my favourite seat. It looks across the ravine which is Troller's Ghyll, home to the trolls and the legendary Barguest – a hound which reputedly howls there at night and which, according to an old rhyme, brought about the demise of at least one sceptic who sallied forth there

From the terraces below the hall there are stunning views across Wharfedale to Simon's Seat.

in search of it, only to be found dead the following day:

> And a dreadful thing from the cliff did
>   spring,
> And its wild bark thrill'd around;
> Its eyes had the glow of the fires below –
> 'Twas the form of the Spectre Hound.

Well, you've been warned! But all I can say is that the view across Troller's Ghyll, with its green velvet sides grazed by hardy sheep, its limestone walls and screes that lead up to the even narrower Jackdaw Ghyll over which the highwayman made his escape from the excisemen, is one of the finest in Yorkshire. There is neither sight nor sound of the spectre hound, but jackdaws are circling overhead, which seems eerily appropriate.

I take the path back down to the Rock Garden and then the car park, where a pair of guinea fowl are skulking through the gravelly dust like two jowly old men with bad feet. Come to think of it, my own feet are aching after that walk up the cliff path. But it was worth it. Oh yes, it was worth it.

Parcevall Hall will do me nicely, when the diocese has finished with it. ⚘

CASTLE OF MEY

Caithness

ROYAL GARDENS CAN be intimidating. Impressive, yes, but also intimidating, especially if they have a regal bearing. You know the sort of thing I mean – grandiose but impersonal. That's probably why I find the garden attached to the Castle of Mey so appealing. Not only does it have the most unassuming and friendly character of any of the royal gardens I have visited, it also has the most exposed position. It stands right on the northern coast of Scotland in Caithness, with nothing except water (the Pentland Firth) between its garden wall and Orkney. The Castle of Mey is nearer to the Arctic Circle than it is to London. In winter the days are dolefully short, but in summer this is a place of paradise where the skies are the clearest blue and the days go on for ever.

Mey itself is the name of the village but Wick is the nearest place of note. I remember hearing once that it had become local tradition to play a game of golf there at midnight on Midsummer Day just to show how good the light was. I wonder if they still do?

This is not the hilly Highland country of Rob Roy, but lower lying land, battered by gales that can reach speeds in excess of ninety miles an hour. It is not the most obvious place to choose to cultivate fruit, flowers and vegetables, but Her Majesty Queen Elizabeth the Queen Mother did in 1952, after the death of the King, and set about restoring the castle and the walled garden that went with it.

At that time it was called 'Old Barrogill Castle'. Queen Elizabeth was staying with friends nearby and so went to visit it and eventually decided to buy it from the then owner, Captain Imbert-Terry.

It has become one of the Queen Mother's stopping-off places in her annual itinerary. She comes here in August and

Stone pillars supporting climbing roses flank the driveway to Longoe Farm, where the Queen Mother breeds pedigree Aberdeen Angus cattle and tough North Country Cheviot sheep.

OPPOSITE *From the stone-built gazebo in the corner of the garden you can see the high stone wall and intersecting hedges that protect the Castle of Mey's garden from the cruel winds that sweep in from the Arctic Circle. Here grow flowers for cutting, flower-beds to sit among, and fruit and vegetables carefully timed for the traditional visits of the royal head of the household.*

One of the 'compartments' where rose beds are surrounded by cockleshell paths. A simple white seat is set against the wall and nasturtiums climb around it. In the corner, up against the gazebo, shelters a lean-to greenhouse.

then again in October and everything in the garden is timed to be at its best while she is in residence.

You'll not see many trees on your way to the Castle of Mey, but then, quite suddenly, you'll come upon a small, gnarled forest, like something out of *Macbeth*, where the sycamores, ash trees and quickthorn are bent and buckled by the wind and hung with silver-grey lichens. A gateway, flanked by stone pillars, presents itself in the middle of them and, by turning up the drive, you will be led to the castle.

Now, although it might not be intimidating in terms of scale, the castle is nonetheless imposing. It was built between 1566 and 1572 by George, the 4th Earl of Caithness and, by the late eighteenth

century, the Mey family had succeeded to the title.

You can spot the castle peeping over the top of the woodland as you begin the approach, but it's still a thrill to see it hove into view at the top of the drive – protected by cannons – its pink sandstone standing out clearly against the pale blue sky. Or grey stone and grey sky depending on what the elements are doing – the colour of the castle seems to change with the weather.

The layout of the castle is in the shape of a 'Z', and there are turrets at the corner of every block. It might not be so frivolous as the castles of King Ludwig of Bavaria, but there can be no doubt that this is a castle and not a house.

Within the lean-to greenhouse not a space can be found – begonias, pelargoniums, salvias and trailing lobelia pack the benches. As with other parts of the garden, the display is timed to be at its best for the Queen Mother's visit towards the end of the summer.

In front of it is an oval lawn, studded with daisies; a gravel drive sweeps up to the front door. On either side of the door is a clue to the ownership: black lanterns with the initials 'ER' silhouetted against the mirrored backing. When the owner is in residence the Royal Standard flutters and flaps from a flag-pole atop the castle.

The things I recall most vividly are the collection of seashells on the window sill

inside the porch, the statue of a black-amoor and a nearby bed of the pink hybrid tea rose, 'Silver Jubilee'.

I remember being at a Royal Horticultural Society flower show in London the year this rose was launched. I was sent to report on it for *Amateur Gardening* magazine, and just as I was poised by the plant with my pencil licked, ready to describe it in my note-pad, a gruff voice said 'Make way please', and a hand gently pressed against my elbow to move me to one side.

'Oh, no, please don't move people', said a voice I knew. I looked up in time to be melted by a Queen Mother smile, and then stood dumbly while she admired the rose.

'Delightful', she said. 'A confection of pinks.' And that is the description of 'Silver Jubilee' as purveyed to *Amateur Gardening* readers – a confection of pinks. It's a pleasant memory.

To the west of the castle is a twelve-foot-high wall made of granite and smothered with the rose 'Albertine'. It seems to be a favourite of the Queen Mother who calls it 'dear old "Albertine", ready to stand anything'. Below the wall grows an assortment of bedding plants and let into it is a wide gateway, again flanked by massive stone pillars, that leads to the sea and to Longoe Farm where Her Majesty breeds pedigree Aberdeen Angus cattle and North Country Cheviot sheep.

Then you'll spot another twelve-foot-high wall and another gateway. This is the entrance to the one-acre garden – a collection of flowers and comestibles that you wouldn't believe could be grown in this wind-blown spot.

The secret of success up here is shelter. Not only that provided by the walls themselves, but also by the network of criss-crossing hedges inside them. These barriers – a mixture of beech, elder,

---

All the walls surrounding the garden are used to good effect. They support many climbing plants, but especially roses of which the Queen Mother is particularly fond. 'Albertine' is one of her favourites.

currant, privet, berberis, fuchsia, hawthorn and Rugosa roses – break up the garden into even smaller compartments, and so prevent the wind from getting a chance to build up to damaging proportions. Most of the time anyway. Ask the head gardener, Sandy Webster, about it and he

Outside the castle walls wild flowers grow on the grassy banks. The scene is pleasant enough in summer, but in winter the days are short and 'Old Barrogill Castle', as it was once called, can be lashed by ninety-mile-an-hour gales.

will confess that he has, on odd occasions, seen cabbages flying over the wall. Now Sandy is not a drinking man, so the flying cabbages must be for real.

Sandy has worked here since 1967, when he came from another of the Queen Mother's residences, Birkhall, on Deeside. He is a skilled gardener and a master of timing. Not only does he produce an abundance of flowers for the garden and the house, and fruit and vegetables for the table, he also manages to get them to be at their best when the royal owner is in

residence and that, as any gardener will tell you, is not easy.

Sandy has his secrets. Some of them you will never prise out of him. Others he will reveal. For instance, he grows soft fruits that crop successively – early, mid-season and late – so he can be sure that one or other of them will come to maturity at the right time.

I asked what it was like gearing up the entire garden to come to its peak during that brief time at the end of the summer when the Queen Mother arrives.

'We are always very happy to welcome Her Majesty to The Castle of Mey', he says.

'And when she leaves?', I enquire.

'We are happy to get on with our work', he replies with a twinkle.

The garden enclosed within these high walls is typical of the kind of Scottish kitchen garden that would have surrounded a baronial castle in the eighteenth century. Look carefully in all these 'rooms' created by the hedges and you will find all you need to withstand siege conditions.

There are plantations of globe artichokes that pre-date the Queen Mother's arrival here. There are redcurrants, blackcurrants and gooseberries that date from her arrival in 1952, and a multitude of vegetables – peas and beans, turnips and carrots, along with herbs – that are all timed for that late summer arrival.

Cabbages and cauliflowers are protected from pigeons by large net cages, and rabbits are not welcome visitors. Not a patch of ground is wasted, and on the walls are trained fruit trees. Manure is brought in from the farm to keep the ground in good heart, but don't imagine that this is a garden only for culinary purposes; it is not. There are some enclosures devoted particularly to flowers.

The most notable one of these is a small knot garden whose beds are edged with sedum and filled with hybrid tea and floribunda roses underplanted with

bachelor's buttons or the tall stems of the yellow-flowered *Primula florindae*. Against the high wall is a wooden bench – a favourite resting spot for the Queen Mother – backed by dear old 'Albertine' and flanked with rampant nasturtiums. They are said to remind her of her childhood, and they reminded me of mine, too, because I couldn't help noticing that they had a little army of caterpillars nibbling the leaves. Heartening to think that we all have the same problem – caterpillars are no respecters of royalty.

The paths in this garden are pure white – they are carpeted with seashells. It is a fairy-tale garden. There are other compartments with border perennials such as phlox and asters, fuchsias and penstemons, as well as old-fashioned shrub roses like 'Great Maiden's Blush', 'William Lobb', a moss rose, and 'Tuscany Superb', that evoke similar feelings.

The problem is that in the Castle of Mey's Garden these old beauties do not seem to thrive. Now there are no doubt some monarchs who insist that their gardeners provide them with precisely what they want, regardless of difficulties in cultivation. But these are generally monarchs who know little about gardening and who are unaccustomed to the vagaries of plant growth and temperament. The Queen Mother is not of their number. She is very probably the most knowledgeable gardener in the royal family and as such regards inevitable failures as a normal part of the gardener's life.

There are two greenhouses in her Scottish garden that positively burst at the seams with colour. The first is a Hartley Clearspan type, and the second a more fitting Victorian-looking lean-to against the north wall. Inside both are great banks of begonias and salpiglossis, cigar flowers and pelargoniums. Billowing kerbs of lobelia tumble over the front of the staging like a well-plumped eiderdown. You are looking here at greenhouses which are in

the great royal tradition – not necessarily in their grandeur, but certainly in the way in which they are filled with flowers. There is not a blank space anywhere. Everything is at the peak of perfection.

In the angle of the garden wall behind the lean-to greenhouse is a stone-built gazebo. The lower floor acts as a potting-shed and, from the flat roof above, there is a great view of the entire layout of the garden and of the coastline. It is a view that clearly demonstrates the skill of the gardener, for outside the wall is nothing but tough grass, rocks and ocean; inside is an earthly paradise.

You might think that nothing in this garden ever changes. In some cases you would be right. There are always the favourite varieties of strawberries and peas, the redcurrants and herbs, but in the flower gardens, while the favourites remain, new varieties are tried every year.

The approach to the castle ends in an imposing view. The stout turreted facade, the flagpole on the roof, lamps bearing the cipher 'ER' on either side of the door and canons on its front lawn all have a distinct regal bearing.

Some fall foul of the drying winds and the salt spray, but others stand up to the severest of all tests and become, in their own turn, favourites.

The Queen Mother is fond of pink flowers and less keen on the stridency of French marigolds than the softer shades of lavatera and shrub roses, and the garden reflects her taste. It is not so much the garden of a queen, but more the garden of someone with a fondness for flowers simply for their own sake. It is a cottage garden – not a garden that sets out to impress, but a garden that cannot fail to do so on account of its position and the personality of its owner.

TATTON PARK

Cheshire

THAT PART OF Cheshire to the south-west of Manchester is really quite smart. If you take the M6 and come off at Junction 19 near Knutsford, you'll pass grandiose detached houses of brick and Sandtex cowering behind high walls. Gilt-finialled gates are the only way into these homes of Manchester businessmen who have clearly done rather well. But one house is grander than all of them. Tatton Park is just four miles from the motorway but a world away in terms of period feel.

It's signposted from the motorway with those brown signs decorated with a flower: the nearest the Department of Transport gets to rusticity. Follow the signs to the official entrance – a broad sweep of drive with a gatehouse and twin double avenues of tall lime trees to right and left.

Now this is the bit I like. The man in the glass booth is jolly as he exacts my £2.50 for the car park.

'You filming?'

'No, I'm just here to look at the garden.'

'Well make sure you see the Orangery – it's been finished now and it's lovely. Ask for Sam.'

So I drive into the car park while sheep safely graze the gently undulating pasture on either side. Ask for Sam he said, but who should I ask?

There is a ticket office – a little wooden chalet with a Wall's ice-cream flag and a sign saying 'Tickets and Information'. Perhaps their information will extend to telling me where Sam is.

The lady in front of me, with a little boy in tow, is trying to find out from the lady in the little wooden chalet the cheapest way of getting in. I have been here five minutes now and she is still not sure whether to have a family ticket, or one that includes the house, or whether to stick to the park and gardens and come back to do the house at the weekend without her little boy, who is right now picking large splinters off the little wooden chalet.

There is a blackboard propped up against the chalet saying 'Wildlife seen in the park this month'. It doesn't mention the little boy, but if I keep my eyes open I could see red kites and buzzards, king-fishers and little grebes on the mere, and swallows, sand-martins, wheatears and chiffchaffs which have already arrived from warmer climes.

If the little boy picks much more wood off the little cedar chalet the lady selling the tickets will find herself in a colder clime. But, at last, the harassed mother

yanks him towards the park and I flash my pass, buy a guidebook and follow in her wake. Oh; I never asked for Sam.

There is a well-worn path across the grass behind the chalet towards the house. A huge fifteen-foot-high wall surrounding what must have been the kitchen garden is straight ahead and, to the left, is a coach yard flanked by a restaurant and a garden shop. Through windows alongside the shop I can see the state coach of the

On the way to the Japanese Garden a bridge is encroached upon by the leaves of gunnera with their prickly stems. By the end of the summer they will be tall enough to walk under, thanks to the moisture at their roots.

The Italian Garden at Tatton Park dates from 1890 and may well have been designed by Joseph Paxton. A statue of Triton, the Greek God of the Sea, at its centre is surrounded by well-tended formal flowerbeds.

Egertons, the owners of Tatton Park until 1958, along with an ornate sled, an ancient fire-engine and a horse-drawn cart that once took picnics to shooting parties. They'd have a Land Rover Discovery nowadays; sleeker but lacking the style of the old brown-painted wagonette.

How to get into the garden? Through the garden shop, says a helpful sign. Turn right past the counter and go through a simple door and you will find yourself in a passageway on whose walls are old scythes and saws, sieves and syringes. A flaking *eau-de-Nil* painted door is flung back against the wall allowing you to enter the garden, and the first thing you will see is a lean-to vinery on your left – the kind that graced any Victorian kitchen garden worthy of the name.

I marvel when I see wonderful old greenhouses like this. They bring to mind the old country estates with their extravagant teams of gardeners ready to tend to every labour-intensive crop that their masters desire.

Above me, on this April day, is a ceanothus weighed down by its powder-blue blooms. There are clumps of daffodils flanking the neatly-pruned rose beds ahead, and shrubs erupt from island beds. Another white-painted lean-to greenhouse occupies a run of high walling to the right where trained peach trees flaunt their fecund stems.

This is the fifty-acre garden of a stately home that was built for the Egerton family between 1780 and 1813 – a neoclassical pile with a vast portico on the south side that affords extensive views of the Cheshire countryside. It is not the first house to be built here – *that* was erected in the late 1600s, but no traces of it survive. Then came a three-storey red-brick house in 1716 and, finally, the present mansion, lived in by the family until 1958 when Maurice, the 4th Baron Egerton of Tatton, died. Thus ended a family association with Tatton that went back to Sir Thomas Egerton, Lord Chancellor of England in the sixteenth century.

You can still see the Old Hall that predated the later houses. It dates from the late fifteenth century and was used by the Lords of Tatton until the first new house was built. Turn left as you approach the house in your car and you will be able to explore the old before the new.

But it is the garden I want to see. I first came here to make a radio programme in the early 1990s and was intrigued by the diversity of plants, the extensiveness of the garden and the changes of mood from one place to another.

From the Vinery and the Peach House a broad path takes you beneath a stout pergola awash with roses, clematis and vines, past wide herbaceous borders (at this time of year you can see the thin and sandy local soil) towards a wrought-iron gate flanked by yews.

Pass through this gate in spring and you are presented with a feast of blossom. The extensive sloping lawns are speckled with cherry trees in their full Eastertide glory and there are magnolias whose branches erupt with waxy cups.

Turn left and you are heading straight for the Orangery. This has been painted in a shade of magnolia and has been fully refurbished. Designed by Lewis Wyatt and built in 1818 it was in a sorry state on my last visit, so it is good to see it crisply restored. Through its tall windows I can spot a central oval bed filled with mimosas and bird of paradise flowers, and all around are citrus fruits in large tubs. There are trellis-backed seats inside the Orangery, and outside great fifteen-foot domes of variegated holly stand guard.

The entrance is at the rear, and this is also the way into my favourite feature at Tatton – the Fernery, originally designed by Joseph Paxton in the 1850s.

Now this is a real treat. Walk into the vast Victorian greenhouse and the atmosphere will hit you like a warm, damp towel – the air is humid to encourage the growth of the towering New Zealand tree ferns and the dense undergrowth of waist-high

The newly restored Orangery was built in 1818 to the design of Lewis Wyatt. It is planted up with mimosa and bird of paradise, and citrus fruits stand about the paths in large tubs.

woodwardia ferns. The tree ferns are hardy in south-western England, but not up here in Cheshire – hence the protection. When they grow too tall they are sawn off, their stumps removed, and the new stem bases replanted in the soil and packed around with bricks for stability. It may sound odd, but it is a technique that has been used here since Captain Charles Randle Egerton, RN, first brought back these tree ferns from New Zealand 130 years ago.

The walls that support the Fernery roof are made not of glass but of brick – they are enormous and are smothered in creeping fig. Above everything is an arched glass roof, rather like that of a Victorian railway station, and there are mounds of moss-covered rocks from which water trickles echoingly into clear pools located below dim grottoes.

Remember *Brideshead Revisited* on television? This is the greenhouse through which Charles Ryder pushed Sebastian Flyte in his bath chair while he clutched his teddy bear. Most of the filming took place at Castle Howard, but the fernery scene in particular sticks in my mind. Stay as long as you like to savour the peaty air and then move on past the ferns and the blue African lilies (agapanthus), the cyperus and the clivias, through the small show house filled with flowering pot plants into the Orangery. The last Baron Egerton liked to read his morning paper here.

Then it is on to the rest of the garden, today past a bevy of schoolchildren with fishing nets about to go pond dipping in Tatton Mere.

Me? I am off to the Italian Garden in front of the mansion to sit on a bench for

The Fernery is one of the highlights of Tatton Park. Designed by Joseph Paxton in the 1850s it shelters a wide range of ferns and tree ferns and was used in the televised version of Brideshead Revisited.

half an hour and admire the scenery. Below the massive portico that decorates this buff-stoned building are terraces that date back to the 1890s. From the balustered balconies the Egertons could admire an Italian-style garden with its central pool and surrounding formal flower-beds edged with clipped box. In the centre of the pool is a water-spurting statue of Triton, Greek God of the Sea, brought back from Venice in 1920 – these Egertons could afford a better class of souvenir.

As the years passed the Italian Garden became neglected but in 1986 was returned to its former glory. Urns decorate the upper terrace and gigantic grassy steps on either side of the central stone flight lead to the flower-beds below. In spring these are filled with polyanthus and wallflowers. The edge of this lower terrace is balustraded and the view beyond, across distant water, is of the Cheshire countryside. Horses and riders meander gently across the landscape and only the drone of aircraft above remind you of your proximity to Manchester Airport.

A man in a tweed jacket strides purposefully towards me.

'Welcome back; it's nice to see you again! How long has it been?'

We try to work out when I was there

to do the radio programme. He asks what I think of the Orangery and we both bemoan the lack of rain this spring and the increasing frequency of the aircraft.

After a while he takes his leave, with good wishes and a wave. I have clearly met Sam, and I never even asked for him.

Time to walk on. I have a guidebook, but I always like to do my own thing and then find out where I should have been afterwards – it adds more excitement. There is plenty of scope to do just that here, and there is a helpful map in the guidebook so you can make sure that you don't miss anything.

I pass weeping cherry trees that look like curtsying crinolined ladies bobbing at

either side of Lady Charlotte's fountain – a tiered pie-crust creation named after the 1st Baron's wife – and head towards a towering yew hedge topped by a topiary peacock and several chessmen. The path leads me by the coronet-topped gates of the old kitchen garden where fruit and vegetables were once grown for the house. Now it is more neglected – parts of it are used as a supply nursery for the ornamental gardens and other areas are simply an echo of their former glory. However, plans are in hand to restore this garden, too. A green bronze bell hangs from the tall brick wall just inside the gate. Once, I guess, it called the men to work or told them it was lunch time, now it hangs forlorn. But this is the only forlorn thing about Tatton, the rest is still vibrant and varied.

Through the yew hedge is the Rose Garden, enclosed by brick walls. A tea house, flanked by pergolas, sits on its top terrace and overlooks the rectangular beds of Edwardian polyantha roses that lead down to the formal pool. The pool was once used for bathing after games of tennis on courts in the Kitchen Garden next door and, in Lady Charlotte's day, the gardeners had to finish work in the Rose Garden by 10am so she could sit out and enjoy the fragrant atmosphere.

From the Rose Garden you can slip through into the Tower Garden with a stout brick-built tower at its corner. How old is it? No one seems to know, except that it was shown on a map dated 1750. The lead cistern below it is dated 1640 and gnarled ivy clings to the brickwork. A small summerhouse crouches in the opposite corner, lovingly restored, with a tiled and pegged stone roof.

A Shinto Temple is the highlight of the Japanese Garden – it was specially imported in 1910. Surrounding the island on which it stands is 'The Golden Brook', a lake made from disused marl pits.

There is an *Alice In Wonderland* feeling as I sneak out through another gate and find myself walking down the main axis of the garden – a broad path with lawns all around and hundreds upon hundreds of ornamental trees, and thousands upon thousands of rhododendrons. Come here in May if you want to see Tatton positively erupt into full flower. Even now, in April, a few of them are showing off, giving a taste of things to come.

I am now heading for Tatton's main show-piece garden, tucked away at the end of paths that wind through great banks of rhododendrons and azaleas. Eventually I come to a sign that says 'The Japanese Garden'. The meandering path leads through tantalizingly fat-budded banks of azaleas and over a hump-backed bridge, alongside which the vast parasols of gunnera are pushing up after their winter rest. Soon they will be tall enough to shelter under in a shower of rain. And then I am there – gazing across tranquil pools towards a Shinto Temple on one side and

Just outside the Rose Garden are some venerable yew hedges topped by a peacock (or is it a chicken?) and some chessmen. Once the hedge was longer, now I expect the gardeners are relieved that there is less to clip.

a thatched tea house on the other. It feels authentic. It is authentic. This garden was built by Japanese craftsmen in 1910 and now it is still as fresh as ever. With any luck you will have a quiet moment to yourself to admire the structure, the planting and the calm atmosphere. I have not – here come the pond dippers! Time to nip off to another path.

The one I plump for leads to the extravagantly-titled 'Choragic Monument of Lysicrates' – a pillared edifice commissioned in 1820 in memory of the Greek storyteller. It is a kind of estate terminus – when you have reached it flop down on a seat to admire the view across the mere and, in my case, take in the eye-lash curling aroma of farmyard manure that is coming from I know not where. To escape it I turn back down the central axis path, past the African Hut and into an inviting-looking path that ducks down among rhododendrons and Japanese maples.

Through the winding paths of the Dell – an appropriate name for this part of the garden – you will come upon the Leech Pool. The family leeches were bred here for the purpose of bleeding those who felt out of sorts. Thank God for antibiotics.

Fed by a fountain, the Leech Pool was at one time used to raise leeches for blood-letting in the household. Today it is strictly ornamental and is surrounded by great banks of colourful azaleas, at their brilliant best in spring.

A family are sitting by the pool – I hope they don't get too near.

Then it's on past the long, narrow maze. No, I don't try it out. It's made of beech hedging which has not yet come into leaf. It would be cheating really – I can see right through it. Then, suddenly, the house is back in view again and I have done the round trip.

There are bits I'd like to see again. Shall I look at the guidebook and see what I've missed? Perhaps an ice-cream first.

So it's back to the little wooden chalet. The mother of the splinter-picking toddler has had the same idea. Will it be a Choc-Ice, Strawberry Mivvi, or a rocket on a stick, or a cone? Will she ever make up her mind?

I decide to leave and shout over her shoulder: 'Tell Sam I've enjoyed it, and I'll see him again next time.' The lady in the chalet smiles wanly. It would have been kinder to have taken her with me.

GREAT DIXTER

Sussex

THEY WERE A group of ladies from Tadcaster. I bumped into them in the High Garden at Great Dixter and they were unanimous in their approval. 'Oh, it's wonderful. You get so used to seeing neat and tidy formal gardens that it's a real change to come here, isn't it? Some of the colour schemes are so amazing.'

These are the sort of people to whom Dixter appeals: people who like to be surprised and amused and who want fresh inspiration for their gardens, rather than playing safe the whole time. Those who judge a garden by its neatly edged lawns, soft pastel plantings and obsessively raked soil will not be impressed. Neither would the owner care for their company.

Great Dixter is the home of a man who is not only a great plantsman and gardener, but arguably this country's finest gardening writer – Christopher Lloyd. His column, 'In My Garden', has appeared in *Country Life* every week since 1963, and his books, among them *The Well-Tempered Garden* and *The Adventurous Gardener*, have become classics.

Christopher Lloyd was born to garden at Dixter and has done so nearly all his life. The house was bought by his father,

OPPOSITE *Outside the Barn the Sunk Garden is awash with a rich mixture of sun-loving hardy and tender perennials.*

Nathaniel Lloyd, in 1910. It was a medieval timbered building dating from the fifteenth and sixteenth centuries. Lloyd engaged the services of a forty-year-old architect who had already made a great name for himself – Edwin Lutyens – and between 1910 and 1912 the house was considerably enlarged. Lutyens also designed the garden, though without the assistance of Gertrude Jekyll (she of the glasses, the boots and the bun), with whom he had already formed a successful partnership.

Northiam is a village on the Kent and Sussex border about fifteen miles north of Hastings on the A28. The approach to Great Dixter is up a country lane which then funnels you into a grassy car park overlooking the Weald of Kent. In front of you the ground falls away in the direction of green fields and wooded knolls, with oast houses peeping through the treetops.

Turning to the house, over to the left is the Horse Pond, its banks furnished with gunnera and its surface part masked by waterlily pads that cradle stars of pink and rose red. Open the old wooden gate, bleached by years of weather to pale grey, and walk down the stone-flagged pathway bordered by long grass. Not until late summer is this rough sward mown, for since the early part of the year it has been a thick rug of wild flowers – wild daffodils and wild orchids, added to by the chequered

bells of snakesheads and the pale blue starry wands of camassias. The spring show will be followed by marguerites, hawkbit and clover in summer, until the mower bites in August.

The timbered porch of the old house crouches at the end of the path, its portals littered with pots, filled on this July day

The house and outbuildings at Great Dixter give a wonderful atmosphere to the garden. Hops were dried in the oast houses at Great Dixter until 1939.

The Long Border is one of the most spectacular borders at Great Dixter. It is packed with a startling colour mixture of border perennials, annuals and shrubs that is ever changing.

with yellow lilies, agaves, blue cornflowers and grey-leafed succulents. There are perhaps twenty terracotta pots, nudging one-another's rims, and inside the porch, underneath its smooth and silvered oak benches, are boxes of canes, empty flower-pots and a battered watering can.

The house, as well as the garden, is open to the public. It is wondrously impressive in its medieval and later timbering; a friendly house – like a favourite old uncle – worn at the edges but good company, and the garden that surrounds it is filled with an assortment of flowers that suggests someone has got at auntie's dressing up box and tried every-thing on.

That someone is Christopher Lloyd. Along with his head gardener Fergus Garrett, he is constantly trying out new plant associations; not just every few years,

but every few weeks. This is not a labour-saving garden. It is, as Lloyd himself points out in the guidebook: 'a high maintenance garden. It is effort that brings reward. If you see ground cover, it's there because, first and foremost, I like it. If it does also save labour, that is an incidental benefit.'

As far as colour is concerned, he says : 'I have a constant awareness of colour and of what I am doing… Bedding allows you the swiftest opportunities for experiment and, if it goes wrong, the defects can be quickly obliterated. The bedding is changed twice or even three times a year.'

So, you see, this is a garden which is constantly changing. Even if its bones date back to 1910, the clothes in which it arrays itself are never the same for long.

The garden surrounds the house on four sides, and by turning left at the front door you will find yourself walking past the meadow garden and into the area that is filled with peacocks clipped out of yew. All eighteen of them perch above a welter of the Michaelmas daisy, *Aster lateriflorus* 'Horizontalis', smothered with tiny

purplish flowers in autumn. Rich purple English irises push up among these waiting daisies in June and July.

The first series of gardens is divided up by yew hedges. As you wander from enclosure to enclosure now, first into the High Garden, then the Orchard Garden, you'll realise that this is no over-prinked showpiece, but a real garden where stock plants are lined out behind foreground plantings. Old espalier fruit trees, their boughs flaking with lichen, are crucified on rustic wooden frames. Vegetables grow in workmanlike rows, and raspberries and gooseberries are tucked up in a rustic-timbered fruit cage, protected from real birds by chicken wire. On the outer boundaries the yew walls are eight feet tall and five feet thick.

Diving through a yew archway I find myself on the broad, flagged terrace of the Long Border. Now this is how a border should really be put together. Backed by a wall of yew it must be fully fifteen feet deep and goodness knows how long.

It is a classic mixed border, where shrubs provide height and bulk, and where perennials, roses, bulbs and annuals are planted cheek by jowl.

In just one patch I noticed, side by side and in this order: orange gazanias, the plummy leaves of Red orach, grey-leafed grasses, royal blue cornflowers, pale yellow flat-headed achillea; then the magenta flowers of *Geranium* 'Ann Folkard' and the electric blue fuzzy flowers of eryngium.

This sort of spectacular plant place-ment happens in every part of the garden at Great Dixter. Strident juxtapositions leave you reeling. It would be dishonest of me to suggest they all work; some of them are howling failures, but far more of them are not, and Christopher Lloyd is man enough to take the risks. Not for him the pink, the pale, the blue and the white in harmonious union.

Walk past the Long Border towards the house and turn left at the round-headed mulberry tree down Lutyens-designed steps. This is where the cultivated part of the garden frays into the wild flower meadow that carpets the orchard. A flagged path leads to the Old Rose Garden where roses no longer grow, thanks to replant disease. This yew-enclosed garden with the long, low, tile-roofed building called 'The Hovel' is now home to a tropical mixture of exotic-looking plants.

Here are purple-leafed cannas, and the giant reed grass *Arundo donax* growing out of a circular raised brick bed. Bananas of the hardy Japanese variety 'Basjoo' make it through the winter here. Orange dahlias, and the purple-leafed, scarlet-flowered variety 'Grenadier', add to the heat, while the lavender-blue-flowered *Verbena bonariensis* has been allowed to push up its head-high stems everywhere at the edges of beds like delicate fireworks. This is a garden at its best in late summer.

Look up at the house now – its coppery tiles, silvered beams and ochre rendering speckled with leaded-light windows are a

The three white cowls of the oast house turn their backs on the Sunk Garden like disinterested Trappist monks.

A mulberry tree stands at the top of the steps where the garden frays into the orchard.

delicious mixture. From here, past Lutyens's open-sided loggia of timber and tile, the path leads you between topiary coffee-pots, complete with handles, into first the Wall Garden, then the Barn Garden, and then the Sunk Garden with its octagonal pool stuffed with water lilies and irises and its flagstone pavement erupting with New Zealand acaenas and Bird's-foot trefoil.

Clematis in abundant variety run up walls, through shrubs and even along the ground at Dixter – the nursery at the bottom of the Topiary Lawn is famous for them, not to mention a wide selection of border plants and shrubs. You can dawdle among the plant frames and pay for your plunder before going home determined to be braver with colours in your own beds and borders.

Christopher Lloyd is now in his seventies, but his passion for plants and his eagerness to try growing them in different combinations shows no signs of fading. To have lunch with him is to be kept on ones toes, to laugh a lot, to be rude about plants and people, and to be hugely entertained. His garden offers the same kind of stimulation. It is a garden worth visiting at any time of the year, though there are those visitors who, on encountering Christopher Lloyd among the beds and borders here, will ask: 'When is the garden at its best?'

To them his answer will always be the same: 'Now!'

CHATSWORTH
Derbyshire

THEY CALL IT the 'Palace of the Peaks', and you really can't argue. It is most definitely a palace, and from all of its windows there are wondrous views of the hilly, often chilly, Derbyshire countryside. From Chesterfield you can travel westwards up hill and down dale through sheep-grazed pasture and, just before the village of Edensor (pronounced Ensor), enter the Chatsworth Estate between imposing twin lodges designed in 1840 by Sir Jeffry Wyatville. Oh, it's a grand entrance.

But if I were you I would decline the invitation at this point and drive on into Edensor itself, a picture-book village with its fairy-tale cottages straight from the pages of the Brothers Grimm. Turn left at the end of the village and enter another world. There are more finely-cropped pastures now, gently rolling and dotted with sheep. Soon the house itself swings into view, perched above the waters of the

River Derwent, and reached by way of James Paine's elegant bridge built in 1762. It really is one heck of a view.

Chatsworth has been the seat of the Cavendish family since 1549 when Sir William Cavendish, having married local girl 'Bess of Hardwick', sold his land in Suffolk and moved up country to his wife's neck of the woods. They built a big Elizabethan house which stood until 1686 when the 4th Earl, finding it 'decaying and weake', began the task of rebuilding. In 1694 he became the 1st Duke of Devonshire (as a thank-you present for helping to bring William of Orange to the throne) so the palace itself is as old as the dukedom.

The river runs north-south, cutting Chatsworth Park in two. The pleasure grounds and gardens are on the eastern slopes of the Derwent valley, behind the house, and the parkland to the west. When you look across to this park from the house and garden you will see the most perfect example of the work of Lancelot 'Capability' Brown. How could this man tell, two hundred years ago, when he planted thousands of cheap saplings that they would turn into what we think of as a classic English landscape? Simple answer: he was a genius. But he was also a wrecker. He swept away the formal gardens and terraces and the pools and fountains that

were built for the 1st Duke and turned them into green slopes dotted with trees. James Paine had already knocked down the old village of Edensor which got in the way of the view, diverted the River Derwent and built his bridge over it. Brown followed on with his own sweeping

Looking through a laburnum arch you can see Joseph Paxton's 'Conservative Wall', a series of protective cases designed for the cultivation of peaches, apricots and other fruits. They echo the railway station architecture for which Paxton was also famous.

OPPOSITE *From the pleasure grounds at Chatsworth the view across the river reveals one of Lancelot 'Capability' Brown's finest creations – a natural looking parkland which is now at its best, 200 years after the death of the genius who created it. Some consider Brown to have been a vandal in sweeping away many formal seventeenth-century gardens, but the 'natural movement' that he pioneered left behind some amazing landscapes.*

From the parkland on the west bank of the River Derwent you can see Chatsworth House through the trees. Begun by the 1st Duke of Devonshire, it dates from the late seventeenth century and replaces an earlier Elizabethan house. High up on the hill behind it is the Elizabethan Hunting Tower.

changes, but between them they created a pastoral scene of undeniable beauty.

These are the sort of views that are underscored by Elgar and Vaughan Williams when translated to the silver screen, so it makes little sense to carp at the demise of the formal seventeenth-century gardens of London and Wise that preceded them.

But do not imagine that Mr Brown swept everything away. Two features in particular date from the seventeenth century – the Cascade and the Canal to the south of the house.

The Cascade can still make visitors gasp with amazement, even if they are well used to the latter-day delights of Alton Towers. Here is a gigantic staircase of water that tumbles down the hillside from a pavilion-cum-grotto that spurts water from its roof and from statues at its base. Here you can find ladies on coach tours at the height of summer with skirts tucked into their knickers soaking their feet in the foaming water as it splashes down the hill. No, this is not Blackpool, and it is not a sight that

makes you curl your lip. It makes you smile. Especially when you remember that this feat of aquatic engineering was completed in 1696.

The Cascade is fed by a lake on the hill above it which was dug out by hand. There are two lakes on the hill. The other one feeds Chatsworth's second water spectacle, the Emperor Fountain, positioned in the canal to the south of the house.

Imagine, if you can, a jet of water 296 feet high which is fed, not by some monstrous pump, but by a moorland stream. The stream is diverted into a lake and then makes its way down the side of the hill through a 15-inch diameter pipe to the canal 381 feet below. The man responsible for this feat of engineering is Sir Joseph Paxton, the designer of the Crystal Palace, and it is to him and his employer, the 6th Duke of Devonshire, that much of Chatsworth's current garden glory belongs.

Paxton completed the Emperor Fountain in 1844 ready for a visit by the Czar of Russia. He never came, but thousands of less regal visitors have marvelled at it over the last 150 years, even if it falls slightly short of its greatest recorded height. I have turned on this fountain with the massive T-shaped key that opens the valve and there is no thrill like it – seeing that monstrous column of water rising higher with every turn, until you are lost in a haze of rainbow-tinted spume.

But who was Paxton? He was a gardener, an architect, a member of parliament and, at the time he was spotted by the 6th Duke, he was working at the gardens of the Horticultural Society in Chiswick on land leased to them by the Duke himself. The Duke poached him and gave him the job of head gardener at Chatsworth. His diary for his first day's work there makes instructive reading:

I left London by the Comet coach to Chesterfield, arrived at Chatsworth at half-past four o'clock in the morning of the ninth of May, 1826. As no person was to be seen at that early hour, I got over the greenhouse gate by the old covered way, explored the pleasure-grounds, and looked round the outside of the house. I then went down to the kitchen gardens, scaled the outside wall, and saw the whole of the place, set the men to work there at six o'clock; then returned to Chatsworth, and got Thomas Weldon to play me the water-works, and afterwards went to breakfast with poor dear Mrs Gregory and her niece: the latter fell in love with me, and I with her, and thus completed my first morning's work at Chatsworth, before nine o'clock.

It was not a flash in the pan; he married her the following year.

Joseph Paxton was clearly no slouch. Aside from the Emperor Fountain, Paxton's legacy to Chatsworth includes the Arboretum, Rockeries and the Conservative Wall as well as the Great Conservatory, a massive glasshouse that was the predecessor of his Crystal Palace of 1851. Alas, the Great Conservatory is no more, but follow the signs to the Maze and you will see just how big it was. There, in a clearing in the wood, are the low walls that supported this gigantic crystal structure. It was completed around 1840 and lasted for eighty years, by which time repair and heating costs were thought to be too great to countenance. It was blown up. Only the walls remain, along with the most electric atmosphere. Stand on

the terrace at the end of this clearing and look over the walls to the maze. It is made of yew and was planted in 1962. At one end of the walled enclosure is a lupin garden, and at the other a dahlia garden – one for early summer and the other for late summer. It will be quiet and, if the sun is shining in June, the sweet scent of lupins will drift up to your nostrils. Can you hear the hooves of the horses that reputedly pulled a carriage through the conservatory, or is it just your imagination? Half close your eyes and

---

The Cascade, built by the Frenchman Grillet, and the folly from which it spills, designed by Thomas Archer, date from 1696. This amazing water feature is fed by a pond high up on the hill, and in summer visitors sit with their feet in the cooling waters that tumble over the steps.

picture the massive dome of glass with its white herring-bone glazing bars. It's a shame it has gone.

The Conservative Wall, back towards the house, still survives. It is a series of massive glass cases attached to a wall where peaches, nectarines, figs and apricots, as well as shrubs unable to survive in a harsh climate, are grown. It reminds me of a rather deluxe railway station, so it comes as no surprise to discover that Paxton designed stations too.

I am picking out my favourite bits of this garden, rather like picking plums from a pudding. There are so many of them, and there is so much to explore that a day at Chatsworth will not seem nearly enough.

It is also one of those rare places that appeals to all the family: woodland walks meander through azaleas and rhododendrons; there is the massive Wellington Rock, a man-made sheer rock face forty-five feet high, that drips with water which eventually finds its way into a little pond;

and children will love the metal willow tree that really does weep if you turn on the tap that is hidden among the rocks. In winter it looks just like all the other leafless trees and has 'dampened' many an unwary visitor.

If the 1st Duke dominated the seventeenth century, Capability Brown the eighteenth century, and Paxton and the 6th Duke the nineteenth century, then the next hundred years most certainly belong to the current Duke and Duchess of Devonshire who have dragged this monolith of a house and estate into the twentieth century with barely an audible scream or a bruising kick. Yes, the gift shop and café are there, but you will not find a lion or a giraffe, a dolphinarium or a funfair. The house and grounds are allowed to speak for themselves.

Deborah, the Duchess of Devonshire, is the youngest of the Mitford girls and, while her sisters might have been famous for their writing exploits (Nancy and Jessica), or their marriages (Diana married the fascist leader Sir Oswald Mosley), or their proximity to famous dictators (Unity knew Hitler), Debo, as her sisters called her, has made her mark on one of England's greatest stately homes.

An astute businesswoman with a wry sense of humour, she and her husband Andrew, the 11th Duke, have kept things moving at Chatsworth.

Woodland clearance and replanting, the establishment of new oak trees each year in the parkland, and the creation of such features as the Serpentine Hedge, the

The Great Conservatory at Chatsworth was designed by Paxton and completed around 1840, only to be demolished eighty years later. Now the site, in a woodland clearing, is occupied by a maze of yew. At one end of the maze is a dahlia garden, at its best in late summer, and at the other end is a lupin garden – in full bloom during June when the spires of pea flowers scent the air.

The Emperor Fountain is one of Paxton's greatest triumphs. Built for the proposed visit of the Czar Nicholas, Emperor of Russia, in 1844, it has a jet which has reached a height of 296 feet. Alas, the Czar never came, but the fountain continues to play.

pleached limes to the south of the house and the the new greenhouses, all date from the present Duke's tenure.

The design of the greenhouse is not to everyone's taste, a monstrosity one visitor called it, but it does house a plant which has strong ties with Chatsworth – the giant tropical water lily *Victoria amazonica*. Paxton was the first to flower it in this country and called it after his monarch: *Victoria regia*. Botanists have since been responsible for deciding that *amazonica* is the correct specific epithet, thereby removing evidence of the gardener's deference to his monarch.

The plant is stunning: massive leaves six feet across that can support the weight of a small child. Beneath them are spines to ward off attacks from below, and deep veins that assist buoyancy. The flower pushes up out of the water and opens white, fading to pink before it closes and submerges to produce seeds. Unbelievably, this monster plant is raised afresh each year from a seed the size of a pea!

Other greenhouses at Chatsworth house camellias, citrus fruits and the like, and outdoors there are herbaceous borders and rose beds and a new kitchen garden which needs time to mature.

I have barely scratched the topsoil of this garden, this estate, this amazing collection of features that reflects the development of British gardening and landscape tradition. The Duchess of Devonshire's book, *The House: a portrait of Chatsworth*, does a far better job and sprinkles the fascinating story with good humour and personality. Not just her personality, but the personalities of previous dukes and duchesses, of comptrollers of the household, estate carpenters and under gardeners. But

then that seems to be the strength of Chatsworth. Any stately home of this kind is bound to present its custodian with seemingly insurmountable financial problems but, while other stately homes have lurched from one crisis to another with family members ever at each other's throats, Chatsworth seems to have retained its stability, as well as managing to keep up with the times.

Thousands of people have dedicated their lives to the Palace of the Peaks – some of them live on into their nineties in the estate cottages – and the old place, in its turn, certainly seems grateful for their attention. ❧

Among the woodland at Chatsworth – and there is plenty of it – are trees of varying ages and a rich collection of shrubs. The current Duke and Duchess have done much to rejuvenate such areas and to banish the encroaching menace of Rhododendron ponticum, *which threatened to swamp everything in its way. Paths had become impassible and the clearance work revealed places in the garden they had never seen before, despite having lived there for some time.*

WOODROYD

Hampshire

THERE ARE TWO ways of looking at it. If I don't include my own garden in a book entitled *Favourite Gardens* then you may be excused for asking: 'So what's wrong with his own garden then?' And if I do include it you'll say: 'What a nerve! It's not as if it's open to the public!'

Well, I did open it once, but we had a thousand people round in two and a half hours and I worried that they wouldn't be able to see the plants for the bodies. I may pluck up the courage to do it again, but for now at least I can tell you about it.

It's a favourite garden, mainly because I've poured so much of myself into it since we moved here in 1981. How does a Yorkshireman end up in Hampshire? It's a long story, but primarily because work dragged me down south and I prefer the countryside west of London rather than east. I would live in Devon or Cornwall as first choice after Yorkshire. Maybe one day I will, but for now I am here with a half-acre garden and around thirty acres of pasture and woodland. I'll tell you more about that later.

OPPOSITE *A topiary duck, clipped out of box, sits among border plants in a huge triangular bed half way up the garden. Beyond it, ostrich plume ferns spring up by the pale blue bridge that crosses the pool and leads to a glade beneath birch trees.*

It wasn't an obvious place in which to make a garden. It was a rough old orchard with apple trees of pensionable age growing on a north-facing slope that has a gradient of one in four. The soil is chalk and flint with a clay cap at the top of the hill. You will have gathered that it is a site with very little going for it. The late Roy

Plants that are good in foliage as well as flower are especially valuable. This is Rodgersia pinnata *which has feathery plumes of creamy flowers and bronze leaves reminiscent of the horse chestnut.*

Hay, gardening correspondent of *The Times*, had a succinct verdict on my choice of terrain: 'You're mad', he said. And that was that.

But you know what it's like; some places click with you and others don't. We stood under an ancient oak tree at the top of the one-acre paddock that rose above the third-of-an-acre 'garden' and said 'Yes; we'll have it'.

Now most people's reaction to a sloping site is to flatten it out. That's fine if your house is at the top of the slope and you can then gaze down on a series of terraces. But if, as in our case, the house is at the bottom, all you would be able to see is a series of brick or stone walls looking like the risers of gigantic steps. Far better, I reckon, to think of it as a theatre: to work with the slope and allow the garden to be presented to the auditorium of the house rather like a raked stage.

The old orchard had certain features that were picked out by the estate agent. There were 'mature fruit trees' (they were falling over). There was a 'rose pergola' (a tumbledown construction of ancient rustic timber held up by an old briar) and there was also a 'stable block'. This turned out to be a black corrugated-iron shelter halfway up the garden which housed a cantankerous old mare that I looked after for six weeks until the owners could move

A small formal garden is edged with dwarf box and surrounded by yew. Within it, standing on gravel, are pots of houseleeks. The rose 'Brenda Colvin' (a soft-pink sort of 'Kiftsgate') smothers an arbour.

Looking downhill towards the house from the kitchen garden, a sundial provides a focal point. I like to terminate all vistas with something definite. Eventually the tall yews will form an archway – with luck!

her into her new Shropshire equestrian accommodation. 'Susie' (for it was she) was a dark brown beast of around fifteen hands and with the stubbornness of a mule when it came to getting her out of the 'stable block' in the morning. I put my shoulder out twice, and on one snowy evening when I had to lead her back in for the night some snow from her hooves flew up on her New Zealand rug and she went ape, imitating 'Silver' in the *Lone Ranger* and rearing high as I slipped over and lay underneath her pounding hooves. I was rather relieved when she left for pastures new – it meant I could demolish the stable and start gardening.

I began at the bottom of the slope, right outside the kitchen window – a technique I commend to anyone starting a new garden. That way you have something to look at close to the house while the rest of the place is in turmoil.

Two banks studded with lumps of marl (a soft, chalk-like stone) were pulled to bits and rebuilt with sandstone around which I could grow alpines. That was the first job. It was winter – a good time to watch the plot and search for inspiration. What to put where? What is in there already?

It's a good idea to watch a new garden for a whole year before you do anything, simply to see what comes up. In the first winter piles of apples left under the gnarled old trees attracted a flock of redwings. The bird life here is rich – everything from green and greater-spotted woodpeckers to goldcrests and blackcaps. I think I'm up to about fifty-seven species by now.

I'm also visited by other forms of life. Deer were a thrill at first, but then they started eating things – roses in particular. Oh, how they love roses. The trouble is they prune them all the year round, not just in March. They can also read labels. Anything with a hefty price tag is, apparently, delicious. In my experience the only reliable way of keeping them out is an eight-foot-high fence. Mine is rather lower than that, but the slope of the garden puts them off leaping it! Moles erupted where I least expected them and rabbits bounded across the paddock on my approach. Grey squirrels occasionally decide to have a de-barking session to rival the deer. But we have survived, and that first year especially was a revelation.

In spring the orchard grass erupted with snowdrops, then daffodils, and then Spanish bluebells. Delicious, but they did mean that a whole swathe of grass had to be cut quite late in the season. Not to worry. I have never seen the point in 'tidying' the garden. I like good lines, but within those good lines I prefer great unruly banks of flowers and foliage.

The only two borders in the garden were above the lawn that topped the rock banks. Come June they blazed into life with orange Oriental poppies. These were stupendous when in bloom, but they go over rather quickly and the borders are dreary afterwards. I worked out a system whereby, as soon as they had finished blooming in mid to late June, I would scissor them off at ground level and plant tobacco plants in the earth around them. They never seemed to mind and kept coming up undaunted year after year until last year when I finally decided that I needed a change and the poppies were dug up for good. That happens in the garden occasionally. It is no use trying to keep it the same year in, year out. It gets boring. Oh, I am patient with trees and shrubs, and with the shape of beds and borders, but within them I like to unpick patches each year and replant.

It took about eight or nine years to get the garden into its present shape. I am not a paper planner – things look different 'on the sod'. I prefer to lay out a garden by looking at it from the bedroom windows and then laying trails of sand along the ground to mark border shapes and pushing in canes to mark the site of trees and shrubs. That way I can see, in my mind's eye, exactly what I am getting. Far easier than transferring an idea from paper to the ground.

I worked up the garden at first, then started at the top and began to work down – which left me with something of an interesting jigsaw problem when the two halves met! I have planned the whole thing as a series of zigzagging paths that turn you to the left and then to the right; that way, as you progress you are offered different views and surprises.

I like a bit of formality, so there are twin formal gardens at the top – one filled with old-fashioned roses and another with a mixture of vegetables and flowers. Between the two runs a path covered with an alley of pleached limes – it's like a green tent in summer.

Where the stable block stood is a small formal garden edged with dwarf box and surrounded by close-clipped yew. There is a bird-bath in the centre and a chamomile path, though moss is doing its best to take over. The beds inside the box and yew are carpeted with gravel on which stand pots of sempervivums or houseleeks. It has a sort of Mediterranean feel. Below this patch of formality the garden is less intricate. The grass paths dart this way and that, flanked by borders that grow a mixture of trees, shrubs and perennials.

There is a pool (artificial) crossed by a pale blue bridge which was hell to carry up the garden. I enlisted the help of four Schwarzenegger-type hunks in the village to help me heave it into position. The shallow pool is full of frog spawn every spring and on a couple of nights the sound of croaking is almost deafening.

From underneath the bridge a snake-like border runs down the garden. It is covered with pebbles (marine cobbles the builders' merchant calls them) and looks like a dry river bed. I am a big fan of pebbles as a mulch. They look great at all times of year, they keep down weeds and they show off foliage plants to perfection.

Two herbaceous borders run across the top of the garden. Phlomis samia *is the yellow-flowered plant and opposite it is a weeping silver-leafed pear,* Pyrus salicifolia *'Pendula'. An urn stands in front of the compost heap.*

What's more, they don't rot away like manure or compost.

Now there's a secret of success if ever there was one – organic enrichment. The soil is so lousy here that I have to help it to grow plants by adding as much compost as I possibly can. I will occasionally lash out on a trailer-load of farmyard manure, but mostly what goes into the soil is what comes out of a hefty compost heap behind the greenhouse.

So full of flints is this ground that the spade goes 'clank' every time I push it into the soil, but I don't remove the stones – there's no point. The plants' roots can grow round them with little difficulty and if I started taking them out I'd never stop. I'd rather mulch the surface of the soil with compost or chipped bark to hide the stones. The compost is more nourishing, but rots away faster, whereas the bark will last a good five years or more if you lay it three inches thick. It really does pay dividends, in terms of plant growth, to lock in the moisture so that they don't go short of water at the roots.

In places the chalk is barely six inches below the surface. There are some plants that simply can't cope with this and you quickly work out which they are. Rhododendrons, azaleas and camellias all have to be grown in pots, but by working masses of compost into the soil at planting time I have been able to grow Japanese maples, witch hazels and a magnolia called 'Merril' which has delectable white starry flowers in early spring.

Topiary I like, so I planted half a dozen eighteen-inch-high yews at the bottom of the garden about eight years ago and began sculpting them into peacocks. I can't understand why some folk think that yew is slow growing. Mine puts on at least six inches every year and now my peacocks are identifiable as such (well, *I* think they are). Yew loves chalk and is a brilliant choice of evergreen hedge with soil like mine. I clip it once a year in August when its growth has stopped – that way it stays in trim throughout the winter. The box is clipped earlier, around Derby Day. It doesn't seem to like being trimmed much later, and browning of the shoot tips can end up being a problem if it is clipped at the same time as the yew.

Favourite plants? Well, I'm a sucker for old roses like 'Belle de Crécy' and 'Leda'. The first opens dusky pink and fades to soft slate purple, and the second has white blooms that look as though they have been dipped in raspberry jam. I love old-fashioned pinks (partly because they love my soil), hellebores and snowdrops, and I have planted a few ornamental cherries because they should love the chalk.

I've become used to the fact that my flowers open a few weeks later than those on the other side of the lane where the gardens slope to the south. A north slope makes for a slow start, but it does mean your flowers are still going strong when those of the folk opposite have faded.

There are bits of my garden that I don't like, but these vary from year to year and I do try to do something about them.

The main path from the top of the garden down to the house passes beneath an alleyway of pleached limes. Another urn (I only have two) and Cornus controversa *'Variegata', the variegated table dogwood, are the focal points here.*

These topiary peacocks have taken about eight years to grow into their current shape. They are clipped a couple of times a year – in late spring and late summer – and should eventually be fully fledged.

Suddenly, a part of a border that was once wonderful will look tatty and it's time for a quick unpick and replant. I wish my grass was less weedy, but then daisies look good in country gardens, and I wish that I didn't have to lug everything up such a steep incline, but then it keeps me fit.

I don't spray with chemicals, except for pirimicarb, a specific aphicide that bumps off the greenfly without harming ladybirds, bees and lacewings, and I use only blood, bone and fishmeal and liquid tomato food for fertiliser. Occasionally I'll apply a moss-killer, weedkiller and fertiliser dressing to the lawn – if it's in a desperate state. A semi-organic garden, it seems to me, is most convenient. All manner of wildlife thrives here and I want to keep it that way.

The greatest treat came three or four years ago when a neighbouring farmer let me buy some more land. I didn't buy it all at once, but in three separate bits – first a bit of wood, then a bit of field, than a bit more wood and a bigger field. We now have around ten acres of mature woodland and about fifteen acres of meadow that is cut for hay. It may sound extravagant, but I would rather be able to walk all over my savings than gloat over figures in a bank

statement. On another four acres or so of pasture we have planted a new wood. Now this is the most thrilling thing of all, partly because we planted our wood in a day.

The saplings were ordered – oak, ash, beech, birch, field maple, wild cherry, crab, whitebeam and hazel – and we invited all our friends to come and plant a few. The spots were marked and the weeds killed in advance. I gave demonstrations to all those who arrived from eight in the morning till dusk. Local ladies administered soup and bacon sandwiches and at the end of the day we had a woodland of over a thousand trees, each one properly staked and surrounded by a plastic shelter. Nobody could believe they had done it and everyone had a lot of fun.

After just two years the young trees (planted at a height of about six inches) were pushing out of the tops of the five-foot shelters, and soon they really will look like a wood with mown rides between the plantations.

The mature woodland has its excite-ments, too. Originally run down and full of litter, we have cleared away much of the Lawson's cypress that clogged it and have started to coppice the hazel to encourage

Well, there comes a time when you have to be honest. I think a garden should be a place touched by humour as well as by cultivation skills. If nothing else, people at least admire the candour – if they can see it for the ground elder!

regeneration. We have had ash logs to burn and are thinning out the canopy so that the bluebells can multiply.

There were old badger setts in the wood when we first took it on, but foxes had moved in – the smell was a dead give-away. We fenced it off from the public woodland that adjoins it and made a circular path around it by felling some of the weaker trees. When walking in the wood we were quiet and kept to the path. And now, what's really wonderful is that the badgers are back. The setts have been redug by powerful claws and there are tracks through the wood, fields and under the fences where we dug out passages for them. As I write this it is February and the badgers will, I hope, be producing their cubs deep underground. We will be watching for them later in the spring, hoping they are back for good. And I will also be hoping that they stay in the wood and don't venture down to my garden! 🌿

POWIS CASTLE

Powys

Is it still possible to feel that you have changed countries when you go to Wales? It is if you travel there over The Long Mynd. Powis Castle is near Welshpool in Powys (yes, the difference in spelling is very irritating) so most folk will approach it from the north, the south or the east. Get close to it by whatever means is most convenient, roughly aiming for Shrewsbury, but then, if you take my advice, you'll start the last leg of your journey from Church Stretton, on the A49, just south of Shrewsbury.

Head west out of the town and you'll instantly start the spectacular climb of The Long Mynd. You're in Shropshire, but you know most definitely that you are on your way to Wales as deep valleys and towering hills appear to the left and right. I am not exaggerating; the view really will make you gasp, and it will be only a matter of minutes before you have to stop the car and admire the scenery.

The sheep-grazed grass gives way to wind-swept heather and moorland, and eventually you pass the famous Stiperstones before hitting the A488.

OPPOSITE *Fat dumplings of yew sit above Powis Castle's hanging terraces and are shown off to perfection by the pink stone of the castle walls. They are thought to have been planted by the 2nd Marquess of Powis in the 1720s.*

Travel numerically now – south to the A489, then west before heading north on the A490 to Welshpool, following the signs to Powis Castle. Don't be put off by the impersonal appearance of the new bypass, for you are about to be hugely impressed by the castle and garden that lurk around the corner.

Up a rough chipping drive you travel, past a sign in English and Welsh (you're definitely in Wales now) between round-topped country hedges of hawthorn and holly. Eventually you'll come upon a little gardener's cottage in grey stone, and then

The Orangery is set into the back wall of the second terrace. Sun-loving climbers romp up its pillared walls, and inside raised beds are planted up with cool conservatory plants – ferns and asparagus ferns, fatshedera and Cupressus cashmeriana.

you'll see the first signs of horticulture rather than agriculture: a superbly trimmed yew hedge, square at all corners and a good ten or twelve feet high, flanking a pair of elaborate wrought-iron gates. Look through these blue gates, with their coat of arms showing a griffin and an

Only when you approach the yews do you get some idea of their size. They sit, like a row of Humpty-Dumpties, atop a wall whose niches are occupied by terracotta pots. In summer these are filled with pelargoniums, fuchsias and a variety of other colourful flowers.

elephant and their finial of a gilded coronet, and you'll have your first view of Powis Castle.

Today the sun is shining and the castle is a rich and ruddy pink, turreted, castellated and chimneyed, glowing against a sky of bluebell blue. Gigantic buttresses of clipped yew seem to be bolstering its walls, and below are the famous hanging terraces

– the finest floral staircase in Britain. You'll not be able to pause here for long – you'll want to be nearer, to see what it looks like close up.

The drive seems to take you away from the castle through parkland furnished with huge old trees and grazed by sheep and deer. You'll find yourself parking on the other side of the castle, the back entrance if you like, and there it towers above you in its red grit-stone glory – stone that was quarried in medieval times from the mound on which the castle is built. Even the lead downpipes are spectacular, each fitted with a cistern at the top which is emblazoned with a Welsh dragon, or is it a

wyvern – that dragon-like beast that seems to figure in the household coat of arms?

There is no time to think; by this point you'll have met another beast, every bit as impressive as a dragon or a wyvern. The sound of rattling quills and humming air warns us of its approach. There, at the entrance to the castle courtyard, stands a beast in full cry – its tail fully raised in defiance and showmanship, demanding to be noticed and attracting the attention of every passer-by. Yes, Powis is famous for its peacocks.

Now I don't know about you, but I can generally be relied upon to make any peacock I meet snap shut its tail with the rapidity of a miffed Victorian lady snapping shut her fan. But not today. The sun sparkles and glints on those iridescent feathers of peacock blue and camera shutters click in appreciation. Only the peahens seem unconcerned, skulking off with a 'pay no attention to him,' kind of look, 'he always shows off in company.'

From here you can either enter the castle courtyard, if you plan to tour the castle itself, or you can look for the little hut a few yards downhill at the entrance to the garden. We sneak a look at the courtyard with its central green and showy statue of 'Fame' but save ourselves, and the view, for the garden proper.

Who lives here now? The last time I came it was the 6th Earl of Powis. I ask the lady in the box.

'It's just tenants and people connected with the castle', she says. 'The 8th Earl is in his forties and lives in Chirbury.'

Shame that. Still, I suppose he finds life a bit more private there, although I bet he misses these gardens. There is nothing, anywhere else in Britain, like the hanging gardens of Powis. When you enter the garden you do so at the western end of the top terrace. Get ready for a great view, a view that opens up and improves at every turn.

On your left are large rocks over which flowering shrubs tumble in knotted profusion. It is spring and rosemary and ceanothus are plastered with pale blue flowers, while down below, to your right, you can see the shrimp-pink domes of *Acer pseaudoplatanus* 'Brilliantissimum' among other trees in more sober livery. Ahead are the hills – the great spine of Long Mountain and then Breidden Hill – and luscious countryside unfolds all round.

It is remarkable when you consider that these gardens were made as long ago as the seventeenth century. I know that the pyramids date back far earlier, but I still find myself wondering how they created a series of terraces like these without the aid of machinery. What is equally remarkable is that they escaped the 'natural movement' of the eighteenth century when formal gardens were swept away to be replaced by a more natural looking landscape. 'Capability' Brown never managed to get his hands on Powis Castle. I'm rather glad.

No one knows who designed the gardens here, though they were made for the 1st Marquess of Powis around 1680. Prominent in the family tree are Anne Parr (sister of Henry VIII's wife Catherine) and Clive of India. The elephant on the coat of arms belongs to the Clive family.

The survival of the garden belies its turbulent history. The 1st Marquess was a Catholic and went into exile with James II in the Glorious Revolution of 1688. He died in France, and the estate was handed to the Earl of Rochford by William of Orange. Eventually the Herbert family returned, and by the beginning of the eighteenth century the gardens were in fine fettle, with an impressive water garden on the site of what is now the Great Lawn below the castle. By the late eighteenth century the gardens had fallen into disrepair and deer grazed on the parterres. But they were once more revived – a revival which seemed to necessitate the removal of the water garden. Ah me!

The twentieth century has seen Powis recapture much of its former glory, and much of that is due to Jimmy Hancock, the head gardener. Jimmy came here in 1972, having trained at Cambridge Botanic Garden and then gone on to work for the National Health Service in Bristol and Wakefield. The standard of upkeep and the breadth of planting is mainly down to him. He's an unassuming chap, with glasses and a grey beard, and I've had many an argument with him about watering and hedge clipping. He always wins. Well, when he tells you that you can clip a hedge just as neatly with electric trimmers as you can with shears you have to believe him when you look at those massive yews. And watering, too. Once anything is established on the broad borders of these terraces, it is left to find its own water – there is no irrigation system and rainfall around here is not high. The thick mulch of manure applied each spring is Jimmy's way of sealing in moisture, and one look at the rude health of his plants shows with no uncertainty that it works.

But where were we? Ah, yes; we've hardly even begun. Flop on the pale green bench beneath a great dome of yew on this top terrace and drink in the view to the south-east. Above you, inside this living umbrella, are a multitude of red-brown spokes. These are the branches that support the overhead canopy that stretches down to the ground, except in front of you where the green visor has been clipped

---

The views from the castle terraces are stunning. The Great Lawn stretches out below, and to the left, through the arches of the yew hedge, is the Formal Garden. Beyond that is the park, backed by Long Mountain and Breidden Hill.

away to allow you to see out across the garden and the valley to the hills beyond.

On the walls that support the top terrace are shrubs like *Abutilon vitifolium* and clerodendrum, and great mounds of silver-leafed cardoons enjoy the rich earth below, along with the feathery grey filigree foliage of *Artemisia* 'Powis Castle'. Tall niches in the walls hold terracotta urns that overflow with tender plants in summer, and the yews tower over them like deep green shrouds.

The yews are the dominant feature of Powis. Thought to have been planted in the 1720s by the 2nd Marquess, they have grown and been clipped over the years to give the gardens 'a sense of age and plump contentment'. Nowadays, shears powered by a petrol generator and a fifty-two-foot ladder are needed to keep them portly but dapper. They are clipped in late summer and stay trim all the way through winter.

Dense planting and thick mulches ensure that the terrace borders at Powis have a feeling of opulence about them. The plants are not watered in dry spells, but the mulching helps to retain valuable soil moisture and so encourage continuous growth.

At the end of this top terrace, when you have gawped at the shrubs tumbling down in front of the castle ramparts, you'll see a fellow with a club beating seven bells out of a beast with countless snake's heads. He is Hercules and his quarry is the Hydra.

Down wide flights of steps you'll travel to the terrace below, at the centre of which is an arched arbour. This is the Aviary. Or rather, it was, for it now houses tender plants like ruellia and correa and the chain fern, woodwardia, within its murky depths. There are half-hardy rhododendrons tumbling from the raised brick bed that runs along the back wall, and the creeping fig, *Ficus pumila*, is scampering up the distempered vaulted ceiling. It's all a bit dank on a bright day, but in wet weather you'll be glad of the shelter.

Outside, on the edge of the terrace, is a balustraded wall from which lead figures of shepherds and shepherdesses, '*à la* Dresden', gaze out over the valley.

The banks that fall away in front of this series of pale ochre archways are of grass, though two narrow borders run to right and left above them. Then it's down another flight of steps to the widest and most spectacular of the terraces – the

Lead statues of shepherds and shepherdesses decorate the balustrade on the Aviary Terrace. They are the work of Andries Carpentière who worked for John van Nost. His work can also be found at Studley Royal in Yorkshire.

Orangery Terrace. You can get a bird's-eye view of it in all its glory from the terrace above, and then go down the steps, awash with shrubs and climbers, to explore it at properly at eye-level.

At its centre is a grass rectangle with bubbles of yew and domes of holly. The Orangery is tucked into the wall behind it, its arched doorway flanked by pillars and the balustrade of the terrace above forming its capping. Ferns and fatshedera, asparagus ferns, *Cupressus cashmeriana* and other cool conservatory plants grace the interior which, at the time of our visit, could do with an overhaul.

No matter. The highlight of the Orangery Terrace is not the Orangery itself, but the broad twin herbaceous borders that run to right and left across the terrace. Packed to the gunwales with hardy herbaceous plants and tender perennials that are bedded out here in late spring, they are the best in Wales.

Huge steel-hooped balloons support domes of clematis, effulgent in flower. Phormiums and shrub roses add height along with fastigiate yews and climbers along the back wall. These borders are

edged with close-clipped dwarf box which adds to their plant-packed feel. Everything from daylilies to sea hollies, delphiniums to diascias enjoy the earthly equivalent of ambrosia if the appearance of this manure-enriched soil is anything to go by.

From this terrace you can see a tree- and shrub-laden bank falling away below towards the Great Lawn, as big as two football pitches, where once the Water Garden spurted in all its glory. And beyond the lawn the Wilderness Ridge – the wild part of the garden.

Walk along the Orangery Terrace to the east and pass through the massive wall of clipped yew. It has the contours of rock and looks rather like magnified moss – all domes and hummocks. Then a zigzag path leads you down the Box Walk, between towering mattresses of box, again all to be clipped, but this time in late spring rather than late summer. Clip box too late and

The origins of the gardens at Powis are not recorded, but there can be no doubt that, thanks to head gardener Jimmy Hancock, the ravages of the centuries have not been allowed to stand in the way of revival.

you risk die-back. Better to clip around Derby Day, which it seems to prefer.

From the Box Walk you get a good view of the half-timbered Head Gardener's Cottage, and of the Formal Garden created in the early years of this century – the inspiration of the appropriately-named Violet, wife of the 4th Earl.

Pyramidal fruit trees, almost a century old, are set in formal rows and, instead of being surrounded by grey dust, they are given spats of golden marjoram and lamb's ears and silver-leafed dead nettle.

There are arbours under which you can sit, and a pergola of vines, again underplanted with golden marjoram. Spiky larch posts play host to clambering honeysuckle, and the ground beneath these, too, is carpeted with an assortment of rug-like plants.

From here you can walk through to two other gardens: the Croquet Lawn, sur-rounded by its own bright borders and with the most stunning mellow brick, half-timbered bothy at one end, and also the Fountain Garden, which looks out through those wrought-iron gates where we first looked in.

A mangy ginger tom sidles across the grass and gives us an old-fashioned look. We take the hint and leave, crossing the Yew Walk and the Great Lawn and looking up at the blush-pink castle and its dumplings of deep green yew. We reach the Wild Garden and the Daffodil Paddock where daffodils erupt in sheets through the meadow grass. Among them are snake's-head fritillaries relishing the damp earth beneath the grass. The air is still and warm and the scent of spring growth is almost tangible.

Climb up above the Daffodil Paddock and turn left and you will find the Garden Pool, which is really out of the garden and into the woods. Kingcups and skunk cabbage dip their toes in the water at the edge of this lake and Canada geese glide nonchalantly across the mirrored surface. Just along the way is what looks like a brick igloo. Now why do you suppose they needed an igloo in the grounds of a castle? Aha, it is an ice-house, and the plaque on its wall explains all:

The Ice House was built in the early nineteenth century. It is twenty feet deep and thirteen feet wide at ground level and was used to store ice collected from the nearby lake. The ice, when properly packed in layers of straw, would remain frozen for up to two years. It was used in the castle during the summer months to preserve food and drink.

Inside is a huge well-like chamber. It's enough to make anyone thirsty. Well, there is a tea shop.

We repair there for Earl Grey and home-made buns and watch the peacock strutting his stuff in the courtyard for another bunch of impressed visitors. The peahens are still treating him as though he doesn't exist. Perhaps, by the end of the summer, they'll have come round to his way of thinking. After all, it's a lonely life for a peahen in a Welsh castle in winter. ❧

HODNET HALL

Shropshire

THE VILLAGE OF Hodnet in Shropshire is long and low and its cottages, which are either half-timbered black-and-white or dusky orange brick, snuggle close to one another at the sides of the main road from Market Drayton. The signpost will tell you when to bear off to Hodnet Hall, and the moment you turn up the little lane you will pass St Luke's Church on your right – a pretty pocket-sized church in red sandstone with a squat octagonal tower. And then, right in front of you, is the stone archway that leads to the garden of Hodnet Hall.

It is a Sunday afternoon in April when I visit. The bells of St Luke's are chiming three as a plump man in his Sunday suit, with a white woolly Arran waistcoat beneath it and a white carnation in his buttonhole, comes out of his shed to take the entrance fee.

'How much?', I enquire.

'You can come in for free if I can have your car.'

OPPOSITE *The four main lakes at Hodnet Hall are planted up at their margins with all manner of moisture-loving trees, shrubs and perennials. The lakes are not natural but man-made, having been constructed from a marshy hollow when the garden was begun in 1922. Today they are the features for which Hodnet is particularly – and justifiably – famous.*

It's a bottom-of-the-range BMW, but I am still rather attached to it, so I pay him £6.20 for two adults plus a guidebook.

The car park is only a short drive from here – a close-mown paddock where plenty of cars far grander than mine have been left to graze while their owners stroll the gardens. The man on the gate had clearly had a lean day.

The car park gives you a taste of things to come: it is edged by handsome country fencing and towered by magnificent beech trees through which you can see the red-brick hall. The birdsong is deafening.

For a change I decide to do as the guidebook says and follow a recommended route, although it occurs to me that if you arrive at a garden which has just opened the best wheeze is to do the route backwards, then you have peace and quiet for the first half of the journey, bedlam in the middle when you pass everybody coming the other way, and then relative solitude for the end of your tour. That's the theory – I must put it into practice sometime!

A meandering gravel path at Hodnet takes us from the car park towards the gravel drive of the Beech Avenue, but we miss the right turn and find ourselves walking up another wide path that runs parallel to it. This route is flanked by magnolias and rhododendrons under which primulas are erupting and bluebells

Steps descend from the Hall to the rim of the Main Pool and they are planted up with a variety of sun-loving shrubs that enjoy the south-facing slope. Stone urns sit at either side of the stairway that leads to the water.

are nodding their azure chains of flowers. A little grass path dives off to the left among rhododendrons and camellias and the urge to follow it is irresistible. We do so, and a breathtaking view unfolds.

Never have I made a happier mistake for suddenly, there before us, the land falls away below banks of berberis sheeted in orange flowers and evergreen domes of rhododendrons about to burst their buds.

Looking over these living bolsters we can see the circular patterned rose-bed on the lower level, the pool beyond it shimmering in the spring sunshine and then cattle grazing a field in which stands a seventeenth-century red-brick dovecot. Immediately beneath our feet are vast cobbles that lead to a tiny summerhouse – the terminus of this pathway to paradise.

Many gardens have delightful corners but this one is a little bit of heaven. Try to find it when no one else is there and enjoy a few moments of purest pleasure with nothing but birdsong and the distant lowing of cows and baa-ing of sheep to break the silence. Intrinsically English though it is, the atmosphere is like that found in Mediterranean coastal gardens where the steepness of the hillside falls away to the sea, and you can sit and sip your drink with a view to die for.

Having found it I hardly want to leave, but eventually we tear ourselves away and retrace our steps to the Broad Walk that runs directly below the house.

Red-brick walls retain the terrace of this ponderous pile, and broad herbaceous borders, filled with soft yellow tulips in spring, stretch out in front of them. The house itself is not a thing of beauty. It is of soft orange brick with stone coins and stone mullioned windows – the blinds are drawn and it looks sightless. It also looks too squat for its length, and then we read that the house 'was reduced in size in 1967 by removing the original roof, tower and top floor to make it more manageable to live in'. Well that much is unarguable, but it did nothing for the proportions of the building. Mind you with views like these, once you are in the house, I suppose it doesn't seem to matter.

The house occupies a raised knoll and the gardens fall away to the south – the ideal situation. The soil is lime free and rainfall fairly high, which makes it ideal for the cultivation of rhododendrons, camellias, azaleas and magnolias. The valley below is sheltered, and in it is the chain of lakes for which Hodnet Hall is famous. From the Broad Walk you can see the Main Pool with its smaller pool, the Horse Wash to one side and then the remaining lakes – Pike Pool, Heber Pool and Paradise Pool – strung out up the valley to the west.

The guidebook suggests a garden walk and then an extended walk up past the pools. We plump for this and find ourselves passing a shaded area on the plan which is designated as the 'Private Garden'. It is. Surrounded by tall and close-clipped yew hedges it is almost impossible to see in. Well, almost. You see, if you are an inveterate Nosy Parker you can't just pass it by. There is a slightly thinner bit of hedge by a summerhouse where we naughtily spy through to see a swimming pool, a Wendy house with net curtains, and another summerhouse containing garden furniture. There are white Versailles tubs dotted

The Broad Walk in front of the Hall has wide, south-facing borders that are packed with a mixture of shrubs, roses and perennials. The soil here is lime free and the rainfall quite high, but hard frosts are rare on account of the stabilising effect of the lakes.

The plantings at the rims of the pools are perhaps at their best in June and July, though there is something to see at all times of year. The gardens here are so extensive – around sixty acres – and the standard of planting and maintenance so high that it is difficult to believe that they are looked after by only four gardeners.

around and a sprinkling of daisies on the lawn. Well, this is the private bit; hence the daisies. Enough nosing. Time to explore the other pools.

There are sixty acres of garden here, all beautifully tended, yet still retaining their great natural charm. They were created by the late Brigadier AGW Heber-Percy with a staff of three men, and are run today by his son, Mr AEH Heber-Percy, and the Honourable Mrs Heber-Percy and a staff of four. It is hard to believe that a garden which is so well looked after has such a modest-sized work force.

The pools look natural, but they are not. The Brigadier excavated them all from what was then a marshy hollow. Today the springs that feed them play their part in keeping the garden relatively frost free, for the pools rarely freeze over – I say pools, but these really are lakes. There are handsome trees on the grassy banks at either side of the valley which, in spring, are covered with golden sheets of daffodils. Snake's head fritillaries nestle among the daffs in the damper areas, and close-mown rides make walking a real pleasure.

On the steep slopes to your right as you walk up this valley of the lakes is a woodland area carpeted with bluebells, and in the rougher grass banks by the water are primroses, celandines and the young shoots of meadowsweet that will open their frothy cream flowers in summer. There are paths to cross between the pools as you pass further up the liquid chain, some of them flanked by the unfurling umbrellas of *Gunnera manicata*, the giant rhubarb.

The topmost pathway, between the Heber Pool and the Paradise Pool, passes underneath tall sycamores, oaks and wild cherries, with wood anemones underfoot. Then you turn left and come back down the valley on the other side of the water. On a warm spring day you will drink in the sweet scent of balsam poplar that wafts down from the freshly-open gooey leaves.

Woodland plants and shrubs cower in the undergrowth and, eventually, you will come to the Water Garden between the Main Pool and the Pike Pool. Here are snaking beds packed with astilbes and Solomon's seal, ferns in assorted varieties, hostas and kingcups and ornamental rhubarb whose leaves are blushing a deep crimson. Here, too, is the skunk cabbage, *Lysichiton americanus*, an arum whose butter-yellow spathes, fully a foot tall, make those of our native cuckoo-pint look minuscule in proportion.

There are seats on which to flop and admire the views down over the water. It is amusing to compare the painted livery of different gardens. Snowshill Manor and Hidcote Manor, both in Gloucestershire, go for a rich shade of blue, while Powis Castle settles for pale green. Tatton Park is into maroon-crimson, and here at Hodnet Hall the benches are deep blue-green. All of them, I reckon, are preferable to white in British gardens. White is for the Mediterranean where the light intensity is considerably higher.

Alongside the grand staircase that descends from the house to the Main Pool are thickly-planted shrubs, serving as a reminder that Hodnet Hall garden has been planted up to be of interest all the year round. Now, in April, there are rhododendrons just beginning to break, with chaenomeles, gorse and broom in full bloom. There are the delectable white wands of *Exochorda racemosa* and the blue powder-puffs of ceanothus pushing up among roses and hydrangeas that will take over the display later in the year.

This is a garden for plantsmen and novices alike, for it can please you however profound or scant your knowledge of plants. And children? Oh, yes, plenty for them, too, as the lad flicking bits of bread into the Main Pool has discovered. Is it pike or carp that are swishing beneath the water as they race for the tasty morsels? Above them, on the surface, glide black New Zealand swans with rosy-red beaks and tail feathers that look as if they have been permed.

The stone summerhouse that sits in the shrubbery alongside the Main Pool contains a plaque which boasts of the garden's achievement in 1985 when it was named 'Garden of the Year'. I can imagine this would surprise no one, especially here where a formal garden is composed of concentric circular beds – the outer beds are planted up with old shrub roses, the next ring with peonies,

Right around the outside of the lakes, and in wooded areas beyond the house, are delightful walks in sun and shade where wild flowers mingle with cultivated varieties. In the woodland, especially, the planting is relaxed and natural looking.

A demure weeping cherry casts its pendulous blossom-laden stems out over the water, and the rhododendrons and azaleas in abundance promise that in June this garden will become a living patchwork quilt of amazing brilliance.

and the central circle with *Hydrangea paniculata*, lavender and caryopteris, so extending the flowering season from one end of summer to the other.

Across from these circular beds is the Horse Wash Pool, though there is no sign of any equine ablutions nowadays, just a deep, cool pool into which water tumbles over rocks. This pool provides moisture for the surrounding soil that supports plump bog plants.

There is always a thrill in bringing home a plant or two from gardens you visit, and Hodnet has the most desirable plant sales area I have ever seen. Make your way past the old Tithe Barn and small paddocks, where cows and Highland cattle graze and young calves sit in the shade of the mellow brickwork, to the Kitchen Garden. Here is a fine example of a walled garden that is still in apple-pie order. Espalier fruit trees cling to the walls and greenhouses are stuffed with plants being grown on. One greenhouse is packed with pot-grown rhododendrons which have reached seven or eight feet tall, and the gentle fragrance that wafts enticingly out of the door is sigh inducing.

Hodnet Hall itself is not the most picturesque of houses, having been cut down to size in 1967 to make it more manageable to live in. But what it does have is a magnificent view over the garden, the lowest of the four lakes – the Main Pool – and the woodland and fields beyond.

Wild duck and a variety of waterfowl populate the lakes at Hodnet Hall, but pride of place goes to the black New Zealand swans with their red beaks and curly tail feathers. They dabble about among the lily pads in the Main Pool in full view of the windows of the house.

Box hedges divide up the beds and a fruit cage prevents birds from stealing the berries. Buy your plants – be they shrubs or border perennials – and make your way back to the tearoom as I did, clutching my bloom-filled potful of exochorda. It's good to discover that this garden's plant sales area sells plants that you have just admired in the garden. Oddly, so many of them these days do not.

Now the tearoom is not for the squeamish. Oh, it looks pretty enough with its black-and-white timbered exterior, but inside it is like a Kenyan game-warden's lodge – filled with hunting trophies from antelopes and gazelles to rhinoceroses and tigers – most of them looking as though they have crashed through the wall at great speed. The sign on the door says: *Please Close The Door To Keep Out The Ducks.*

If a duck took one look in here it would be out through that door like a flash. But it would probably come back, as I suspect most visitors do. Having seen Hodnet Hall Gardens at one season you'll want to see it at another. I can't wait to return in summer when the trees are in full leaf and the water gardens are at their best. I might even swap my own garden for this one. But not my car. I hope it's still there. ❦

HELMINGHAM HALL

Suffolk

I HAVE NEVER BEEN much of a mover. Born at granny's, my parents moved twice and I have moved twice, so I have lived in just five different houses – hardly the sign of a restless soul. I have friends in the air force who have lived in four times as many places in the same length of time. What they would make of the Tollemaches I do not know – Helmingham Hall has been their home since 1510 and they have lived in Suffolk since shortly after the Norman Conquest. Their name was originally spelt *Talemache*, meaning 'purse bearer' and it is recorded that Hugh Tollemache was Purse Bearer to Henry I.

Suffolk is a county I like – it rolls very gently. There are one or two things you could call hills – enough to prevent the county from appearing fenlike and flat – but there is nothing that could be too taxing on the bicycle pedals.

OPPOSITE *Helmingham Hall is the kind of moated manor house the Englishman dreams of when he is abroad. Built of mellow brick and completed in 1510, not only is the house surrounded by a moat, but the garden is, too. The Tollemache family continue to live in the house that their ancestors built.*

Helmingham is a village to the north of Ipswich and east of Bury St Edmunds and is surrounded by lush farmland and presided over by the Hall. The Hall's own parkland is lush, too, and peppered with English oaks that were pushing their way up from acorns when Harold sat on his horse with his hawk in his hand in 1066. They are old. You will park under them when you visit – not too close if you value your car – and then tramp the gravel drive and the sheep-spattered turf toward the Hall itself. The first thing you will notice is the silence – no aeroplanes, no distant hum of traffic, just the plaintive bleating of sheep and lambs and the songs of a hundred different birds.

Over to your left, through the trees, rises the buff-stone, sixteenth-century tower of St Mary's Church, reached by a grass-topped stone bridge. Right in front of you, in the middle of this deer park, is an elegant red-brick hall, built around its own courtyard and surrounded by a moat. Helmingham Hall is everything you could ask for in a house. Completed in 1510, and visited by most monarchs from Elizabeth I to Elizabeth II, the bricks are dusky terracotta, there are Tudor gables at the

A statue of Flora, the Roman goddess of flowers, stands in the centre of the Rose Garden. Completed in 1982, this garden is planted up with old-fashioned shrub roses – Albas, Gallicas, Damasks and Bourbons, Centifolia and Moss roses – and underplanted with lavender, geraniums, violas, lady's mantle and other ground cover plants.

corners, drawbridges that can be raised and lowered, towering chimneys that seem to be topped with onion domes, and a garden that will make you sigh with pleasure.

Walk from your car in the direction of the Hall and you will find yourself approaching it from the south-east. You can peer over the encircling brick wall into the moat – a weedy stretch of water, but furnished with fish that dart to port and starboard in search of midges on a summer's afternoon. Look carefully; there is a six-foot-long catfish in there somewhere. It sounds like a classic fisherman's tale, but it was told to me by Lady Tollemache so it must be true. The

fish was put into the water in 1953, so perhaps forty-odd-year-old catfish are six feet long.

The sloping banks of this protective circuit of water are awash with cowslips in spring, followed by pink clover and marguerites as spring turns into summer. Dragonflies and damsel flies cruise across the still water. The sun warms the russet brickwork with its dark plum diamond pattern as you round the corner, past the white-painted filigree bridge and drawbridge towards the Walled Garden.

I know of a number of houses with their own moats, but very few moated gardens. Well, at Helmingham Hall there

are both – the garden has one too. This pre-dates that of the house; it is thought to be Saxon, from a time when the garden was a pallisaded cattle enclosure. The raised grass path between the two moats is flanked by domes of golden yew, and because the mower has travelled wider

---

The Knot Garden has neat beds of clipped box – two of them show the fret pattern that can be seen in the brickwork of the hall and the family coat of arms, and another two incorporate the initials of Lord and Lady Tollemache – a 'T' and an 'A'. They are interplanted with a rich mixture of herbs and lead the visitor through to the Rose Garden.

between these living bollards, the effect is of a gently scalloped path.

The moat surrounding the hall is to your right now, and that surrounding the garden is to your left – filled with sweet flag and water lilies. And then, when you are plumb in the centre of this side of the Hall, you can turn left and see down the centre of the Walled Garden through a tall pair of wrought-iron gates that allow you to enter its sheltered confines.

Don't rush it. There are things to see before you succumb to the walled temptation. Just across the garden moat is a formal garden – a sort of overture to the Walled Garden – which comprises twin quartered beds of clipped box infilled with aromatic grey cotton lavender and centred by wide-mouthed urns. The formal beds are surrounded by a border of hybrid musk roses – handsome, hefty shrubs which make good garden plants where they have room to cast their wands of flower. They bloom continuously through the summer, have powerful fragrances and good-sized flowers in a wide range of colours. Here you will find treasures like the single rich pink 'Vanity' and creamy-coppery 'Buff Beauty', as well as rarities like 'Thisbe' and 'Nur Mahal'. The collection was begun by the last Lady Tollemache and is being continued by the present one.

At the feet of these roses – at their very best in late June and early July – is a thick rug of London pride retained by a kerb of lavender and mid way along each of these borders that run to either side of the Walled Garden gates are mulberries, leaning out over the grassy path. Inhale the fragrance of the roses and lavender and then pass through the central gateway to be enraptured by what seem to be twin herbaceous borders that run down the Walled Garden as far as the eye can see.

But this is really a neat trick. What you are looking at are the ends of a series of rectangular beds, with taller perennials at the back and shorter ones to the front, and

with climbing roses like the pale pink 'New Dawn', coppery 'Albertine' and rich purple-crimson 'Gruss an Teplitz'. But behind these flowers are vegetables and fruits occupying the rest of these enormous beds. This, in reality, is a Kitchen Garden – one of the best in the country.

The walls were built in 1745 and, 250 years on, the soil is in good heart; twenty-five decades of manure have had their effect on the loam of Helmingham. Roy Balaam, the head gardener, is now in his early fifties, but he has been a gardener here since he was fourteen. He refuses to use a rotavator; instead, all the Kitchen Garden beds are dug by hand. Including Roy, there are three and a half full-time gardeners here, and that allows for Lady Tollemache who counts herself as a part-timer. The standard of maintenance is high, especially among the vegetables where beds of asparagus and globe artichokes jostle with more basic fare like broad beans and beetroots.

On the banks of the garden moat, alongside the Apple Walk, sheets of daffodils decorate the greensward in spring, along with cowslips and primroses. This moat is thought to date from Saxon times when the area was used as an enclosure for cattle.

Nowhere do you get the impression that this is a Kitchen Garden cultivated just for show. There are long glass cloches to bring crops along early and thick mulches of straw around the strawberries. The walls are clad in espalier fruit trees, and no square foot of the rich black earth is unused. But there are decorative features, too. Running at right angles to the main central path are two tunnels made of iron hoops. Over them are trained runner beans, sweet peas and, unusually, gourds. These cucumber relatives are planted out at the foot of the iron supports each spring when danger of frost is past, and the long and questing stems are trained up one side, over the top and down the other. In late

A seat, designed by George Carter, offers a chance to relax at the end of one of the archways in the Kitchen Garden. Here grows a wondrous mixture of flowers, fruit and vegetables, and the archways support sweet peas, runner beans and gourds. This part of the garden is tremendously attractive but also hard working.

The older Rose Garden to the west of Helmingham Hall is planted up with hybrid musks and edged with a wide kerb of 'Hidcote' lavender. The underplanting is of London pride. A stone eagle sits atop the pillar at the end of the old brick wall.

summer these succulent vines are hung with the yellow, orange and green flagons of the gourds, so that walking down them is like passing beneath an arcade hung with Chinese lanterns.

There are borders directly underneath the walls, too, where different crops can be given the aspect they prefer, and there is space for herbs and perennials that are being grown on, and annuals for cutting for the house. And they do get cut.

As I walk into the Walled Garden, so the butler walks out – his green baize apron covering a crisp white shirt and black tie, and under his arm a trug basket full of flowers.

Explore the Kitchen Garden properly before you exit at the far end. You then have three choices, the first of which is to go straight ahead, around the tennis court and dawdle among the purple-flowered spotted orchids, the field butter-cups and the marguerites that carpet the orchard floor. Take a look at the green-houses here – old and venerable brick and white-painted structures, and a new aluminium one that shelters a collection of conservatory plants displayed like jewels in a trinket box – everything from plumbago and pelargoniums to angels' trumpets (daturas) and sparmannia.

In spring, turn to the left, and then left again, to come up the outside wall of the garden past the Spring Border. It was the designer Gertrude Jekyll who advised gardeners to devote beds and borders to just one season of the year, and she would have been well pleased with this one – first there are tulips, then there are bearded irises, peonies and pyrethrums, red-flowered valerian, and a wall that is hung with swags of clematis, honeysuckle and other early-flowering climbers.

Outside the opposite wall of the garden is an Apple Walk – an avenue of mixed varieties that will lead you toward the north-west side of the Hall and the refreshments of the Coach House tearooms. It is on your way there that you will spot a neatly-painted sign which says 'Herb and Knot Garden'.

This garden, laid out in 1982, is a treasure. First there are four 'knots' of close-clipped dwarf box, reflecting the pattern in the Tollemache family coat of arms, and the initials 'T & A' of the present Lord and Lady Tollemache – Tim and Alexandra. The interstices are planted up with herbs – purple sage and lilac-flowered chives, Turk's-cap lilies and clove pinks – the aroma rises to your nostrils on the warm summer air.

Then come two beds planted up with the candy-striped 'Rosa Mundi', under-planted with forget-me-nots and catmint

– altogether a cracking and distinctive colour combination.

Ahead of you now is a statue of the goddess Flora on a circular carpet of golden thyme and surrounded by beds that are simply billowing with old-fashioned shrub roses. They are trained (or are they, for there is no sign of support) into floral mounds that shower their blooms from above head height, right to the ground. The secret lies in the support system – Helmingham Hall's own rose support which comprises a central steel post, fitted with a kind of maypole system of wires pegged down to the ground. Positioned in the centre of a youthful shrub rose it allows the young stems to be tied in, so preventing them from bowing down and pulling the bush open after heavy rain. It really does seem to work, and the foliage and flowers make it invisible in summer.

Here are all the old roses with those delectable names: the Damasks and the Bourbons, the Chinas and the Centifolias, the Moss roses and the Gallicas and the hybrid perpetuals. You can easily lose your head among the flowers in this garden and end up emerging almost drunk with the pleasure of scent from such beauties as 'Fantin Latour', 'Souvenir de la Malmaison' and 'Königin von Dänemarck'. Their names alone should make you want to grow them and, if that's not enough, their perfume and the purity of their petals will seal the deal.

This garden is enclosed by tall yew hedges, but a window has been cut into the end wall to allow you to look out over a long pool to the deer park beyond. But the tearoom beckons, and you can get to it by walking out of the Herb and Knot Garden towards the Coach House down a path

lined with mop-headed specimens of *Pyrus nivalis* – a silver-leafed pear that lends itself well to such training – whose trunks are enclosed in squares of clipped box.

A Burmese cat yowled at me from the doorstep of the Coach House and a liver-and-white spaniel ran barking along the bridge to Helmingham Hall. He was just in time. As he neared the welcoming portals of dusky brick, the drawbridge was raised for the night, just as it has been every night since 1510. I think if I had a house like this, I'd be happy to live in it for five hundred years.

At either end of the Kitchen Garden are wrought-iron gates supported on pillars that are topped with winged horses. The walls surrounding the Kitchen Garden date from 1745 and outside them are borders planted to be of interest at various different times of the year.

LANHYDROCK

Cornwall

THERE WAS A time when a journey to Cornwall could be a real ordeal, especially at holiday times. Ask any driver who has driven through Cornwall what the name 'Indian Queens' means, and he will not say Minnehaha and Mrs Sitting Bull, he will say 'traffic jams'. You could sit for hours in your motor on a sunny day, near the village of Indian Queens, steaming in the heat while the children persisted in asking, through mouths stuffed with crisps, 'Are we nearly there?' A trip to Torremolinos in the overstuffed economy section of a charter flight would be a doddle in comparison. But now Indian Queens and neighbouring Fraddon have been bypassed and the journey down the A30 to Penzance is a dream. And wild and woolly Cornwall is a dream, too. I love it.

Lanhydrock is one of the delights on the way to my annual stamping ground of Sennen Cove and Penwith – it's just off the A30 between Bodmin and Lostwithiel. The brown 'Lanhydrock' signs lead you away from the main road and the fast traffic,

down a series of country lanes. That's better. Peace at last. Birdsong and breezes.

Then you turn into a gravelly car park which has a small plant centre attached. Re-cross the country lane on foot to enter the grounds proper. You'll buy your ticket at the smart pavilion, and the ladies behind the counter might just persuade you to join The National Trust. Oh, go on. It really is worth it. I worked out that if you visit just five properties in a year you've covered your membership costs, and the pleasure is immense. Well, it is for me, especially at Lanhydrock.

From the entrance pavilion you'll walk downhill into the sheltered valley for around half a mile, tramping on the grassy slopes next to the wide drive between an avenue of oaks. You'll overlook parkland where cattle and sheep graze among the mature oaks and beeches. If you want a peaceful spot you'll find it here.

Eventually, to the right, a small church tower comes into view, backed by tree-clad hills. In front of it you'll soon see the house – pale grey stone, with long, grey slate roofs – arranged on three sides of a central courtyard. Originally built in the seventeenth century, it was remodelled in the mid-nineteenth century, ravaged by fire in 1881, and then largely rebuilt. It sits calmly now behind a formal garden which is surrounded by low, castellated walls in

The upper slopes of the garden at Lanhydrock are richly planted with shrubs. Keen plantsmen will dart in and out of the undergrowth every few yards as yet another treasure comes into view. The acid soil means that rhododendrons, camellias and magnolias thrive here.

which is set a handsome gatehouse of buff-grey granite topped by a feast of pinnacles. It's a little gem. The oldest building at Lanhydrock, it was completed in 1651 by John, Lord Robartes, 1st Viscount Bodmin and 1st Earl of Radnor.

Lanhydrock remained home to the Robartes family until 1953 when it was eventually handed over to The National Trust. Inside you can escape into a fascinating Victorian world of elaborate

OPPOSITE *The gatehouse is the oldest building at Lanhydrock, dating from 1651, and acts as the formal entrance to the Formal Garden with its twenty-nine crisply-clipped Irish yews and beds of roses. Over the rooftops of the stable yard and its clock the view of the Cornish countryside seems to go on for ever.*

wash-stands and leather luggage, bulging linen cupboards and kitchens agleam with polished copper. The rooms are laid out as though the family were still in residence with the minutiae of everyday Victorian life as much in evidence as the usual grand furniture and paintings. But I'm here for the valuables outside.

The Gatehouse is Lanhydrock's finest embellishment and will lead you into the Formal Garden. But walk on, round the corner and enter the garden through the stable yard, first looking down the double avenue of beeches to the valley of the River Fowey. This avenue was originally planted with sycamores in 1648 and one or two of them are still there. There are even better views as you climb the slopes of the garden behind the house, but that's in a while.

The Long Border, which leads up to the Higher Garden, is well planted with hostas which provide ground cover to magnolias, osmanthus and rhododendrons.

For now, go round through the stable yard, past the Stable Bar Café and through a huge studded door into the Formal Garden. Here you'll find lawns of lime green velour arranged in gentle terraces with symmetrical beds of roses cut out at their centres, and cylindrical, flat-topped Irish yews set like chessmen at the corners. The bronze urns in this garden originally came from the Château de Bagatelle in Paris, which was once the home of Marie Antoinette. So how exactly did they come to be here? They were 'acquired' by Frances Gerald Agar-Robartes, the 7th Viscount Clifden. On his 'Grand Tour' perhaps? A touch of the Elgin Marbles? I was curious, so I looked him up in the guidebook. His

dates are given as 1833-1966. It must have been a long and fulfilled life – all 133 years of it. Oh, come on; it doesn't have to be a misprint. And the truth about the urns? Ah, the Marquis of Hertford lived at Bagatelle in the mid-ninteenth century and then came here via assorted subsequent owners. All quite above board and nothing to raise an eyebrow at at all. Except his age.

Behind the house stands the granite Church of St Hydroc, dating from the fifteenth century. St Hydroc came to Cornwall from Ireland as a missionary with his brother Madron. The church was at one time linked to the Augustinian Priory of St Petroc at Bodmin.

But back to the gardens. As is the case with so many country estates, the original formal gardens that occupied this site were replaced in the eighteenth century with 'countryside' that came right up to the house. But in 1857 the Formal Garden was reinstated to its current form.

A circle of grass occupies the centre of the courtyard surrounded by the three wings of the house, and climbers run up the walls, among them a venerable *Magnolia grandiflora* and a climbing hydrangea-like *Schizophragma integrifolia*, whose cream blossom speckles the sallow stonework in late summer.

The gentle terraces of the Formal Garden rise once more by the side of the house to a more elaborate parterre – an intricate pattern of beds planted up with Semperflorens and tuberous begonias. Now I know the Victorians were keen on loud colours, but I can't quite work up any enthusiasm for these. They seem both anachronistic and far too strident.

A border stuffed with agapanthus, geraniums and fuchsias runs along the side

of a stone wall now, and behind it, reached by a flight of steps that lead through an iron gate, is the Church of St Hydroc. This is a fifteenth-century church of grey granite with a squat tower, a main chancel and two side aisles. Walk on up the hill to the right of the tower, passing through the quiet Cornish churchyard where foxgloves, campions and fuchsias grow under a massive chestnut tree, and where departed Cornishmen and women lie underneath the rolling waves of turf, their battered headstones a testament to the chilly weather in this part of the West Country. Frosts can come to Lanhydrock until the end of May, but at least the acid soil is hospitable to the plants for which it is most famous – the magnolias, camellias, rhododendrons and azaleas that make this a spring garden *par excellence*.

The further you get from the house at Lanhydrock the more exciting is the journey. Well, it is if you're an inveterate plant hunter like me. In some gardens the formal areas are the ones to treasure, but here I feel a need to hurry past them, for it

In the Woodland Garden, on the upper slopes of the hill above Lanhydrock, the feeling is much more that of native British woodland. Bluebells carpet the floor beneath the lofty trees that remain after the devastation caused by the gales of January 1990.

is the woodland that holds the greatest delights – in spring, in early summer and in autumn when the tints are startling.

Pass through the Herbaceous Circle – a quartered circle surrounded by a tall yew hedge and planted up with euphorbias, rodgersias, montbretias, macleaya, tree peonies and delphiniums – and head uphill past the Long Border where hostas elbow one another for space.

At the end of the Long Border you'll come to a sunken stone well-house where water drips plangently into a deep pool. This is the Holy Well – a spring originally used by the monks of St Petroc's Priory at Bodmin. Next to it is the Thatched Cottage, lived in until 1885 but now used as a shelter from the rain or for picnics in foul weather. The walls inside are decorated

The Parterre with its brilliant spring bedding, replaced in May and June with a summer show. The bronze urns at the centre of the display once graced the gardens of Marie Antoinette's home in Paris. They were later acquired by the 7th Viscount Clifden. Similar urns still decorate the gardens at Versailles.

with old gardening tools: scythes and sickles, rakes and hoes, a besom and a pitchfork and assorted evil-looking blades – and there is an ingle-nook fireplace at one end on which rests a potful of pheasant feathers, a wooden duck and some bottles, all seen in the watery light that filters in through the leaded windows. No, this is not the ultimate excitement. That comes next.

Come out into the sunshine and blink, then head uphill through a tunnel topped with foliage. At least it is foliage that furnishes it in summer; in spring it is smothered with waxy white goblets that are flushed with pink, for this is the magnolia tunnel, decorated with the *Magnolia* x *soulangeana* hybrids 'Lennei' and 'Rustica Rubra'. A real delight.

What you'll be noticing now are the trees around you – vast trees. But these are not just sycamores and oaks and limes, they are much more exotic. These giants are magnolias and maples, ostrya and nothofagus, taxodium and *Parrotia persica* – the Persian iron wood that starts to take on ruddy autumn tints as early as late July and August. There are vast spreading specimens of *Cornus kousa* from China which are bedecked in June with creamy stars as big as your hand and which blush to ruddy crimson at the edges.

Above the tunnel are magnolias that grow unrestricted to fifty feet and more. This is the towering *Magnolia hypoleuca* with its cup-shaped creamy-white blooms that smell of ripe water melons when they open in June and July.

There are other magnolias to discover as you wander around the paths that now climb the side of the valley above the house. Beneath the fresh green leaves of *Magnolia sinensis* hang peals of pure-white five-inch bells centred with purple and green clappers, simply forcing you to look upwards and miss your step. You'll have to come earlier in the year for the massive pink cabbages of *Magnolia campbellii*. They open on tall trees that are bare of leaves in February and March and are devastating against a blue spring sky. But being here at any time of year is like being in wonderland.

Everywhere there are gigantic mounds of rhododendrons in innumerable variety. They fill banks and hollows between the trees and they occupy great lengths of border in their own right. Purple, pink, white, rosy red or primrose yellow, held above leaves that are dark green or decorated with russety felt. They flower in profusion during April and May ensuring you of a gasp at every turn. Even in late June a few of them are still sputtering on.

Just remembering all these beauties makes me want to revisit the place. And there is no worry that I'll not be able to find the trees I sighed over: the plan of Lanhydrock that can be bought at the pavilion shows you just where to walk in the grounds, and what you will encounter on each section of path. Treat it like a treasure map, as I do, and wander around clutching it and diving into the bushes here and there to turn up new treasure trove. Paths zigzag up and down the slopes above the house, and every now and then, as you emerge from your forays, you'll see the wondrous views down the valley of the River Fowey.

Crinodendrons, twenty-feet tall and as much wide, are positively dripping with their raspberry-pink bell flowers on this June day. Electric blue hydrangeas flank the path now, the surrounding fresh-mown grass making a rich green rug that shows them off to good effect. Below them are the rooftops of the house, the deer park and the valleys beyond.

Climbing higher up the path you'll pass through iron gates and enter the woodland proper. There is no mown grass here, just shafts of warm sunlight stabbing down through the canopy above and illuminating the leaves of rhododendrons – some of them nearly two feet long on *Rhododendron sinogrande* – planted as thickly on the woodland slopes as the rest of us plant lupins in a border. Ferns push up through the leafy loam, along with blue alkanet, cocksfoot grasses and the odd clump of stinging nettles. The trees that tumbled like flayed giants on these hills in the January gales of 1990 have now been replanted and the new visitor will barely notice they are gone.

From up here on the hill the views are best of all. You can see across the first valley, enclosed by woodland, to the fields beyond and the hills rising in the distance, one on top of another, until the farthest horizon is a feint blue-grey. There's not even the sound of a bleating sheep. All is still and silent. I've been lucky with the weather yet again. Perhaps you will not. But even at less fairer times the upper slopes of the garden at Lanhydrock offer the rich pickings of more than a century of gardening and plant collecting.

There are thirty acres of goodies here, and they are not just for the keen plantsperson. The whole layout of the paths on the valleyside makes for a spirit of adventure. Some of the trees here were planted in the seventeenth century and new ones are still being planted to make sure that Lanhydrock goes on being an irresistible draw to gardeners like me. But even if you visit Lanhydrock in the company of someone who thinks that one tree is very much like another, by the time they have climbed the side of this lush Cornish valley, they could well see things rather differently. I hope so. ❧

The Herbaceous Circle, with its collection of border perennials, is overlooked by the 'Tithe Barn'. It is a Victorian edifice made from the remains of the original monks' house, and its gable contains a stone archway removed from the Church of St Hydroc when the building was extended in 1886.

ROYAL BOTANIC GARDENS

Kew – Surrey

'LETTERS AFTER YOUR name; that's what you need', said the blokes in the Parks Department where I started work. Here was a lad who had left school at fifteen to serve a five-year apprenticeship in a Yorkshire nursery – letters after my name seemed highly unlikely. But they had my career mapped out for me and it would have been churlish not to follow their suggested route. So I took their advice and went to horticultural college for a year before applying to be taken on for a three-year course that would lead to a diploma in horticulture at the Royal Botanic Gardens, Kew. If I was accepted, and if I passed all the exams, I would be a Dip. Hort. (Kew).

The interview was tricky. There were three men and a woman behind a large oak table: the curator, the supervisor of studies, an assistant curator and a secretary. I sat on a chair in front of them, in my new grey

OPPOSITE *The parterre in the Queen's Garden at Kew with an ornamental well-head at the centre and a pool with a fountain at the end. The hedges are clipped annually – a job I carried out for several years to supplement my meagre student's pay!*

suit, trying not to tremble while they fired off a series of questions designed to test my suitability as student material. They had

The famous Palm House is the work of Decimus Burton and engineer Richard Turner and was built between 1844 and 1848. It houses a wonderful collection of palms and rare cycads, and beneath it there are aquariums full of fish and aquatic plants.

hundreds of applicants they said. And they only took on twenty students.

'What do you think of the rock garden at Wisley?', one of them asked.

I said I quite liked it.

'Don't you think there's rather a lot of rock in it?'

'Yes, I suppose there is', came the lame reply.

Apart from a question on the best time to prune caryopteris (the assistant curator disagreed with my answer) I don't remember much more. I went home on the train, a bit crestfallen.

A few weeks later I got a letter telling me I had been accepted, and my parents bought me a transistor radio.

So I turned up on a September morning when the *Anemone japonica* was in flower, and now whenever I see that plant in bloom I think of Kew.

There are 300-and-some acres of garden making up the scientific institution known as The Royal Botanic Gardens, Kew. At one time you could get in for a penny; now it costs several pounds, but when it comes to value for money, this place is tops.

It's difficult knowing where to begin describing its delights; there are so many of

The Princess of Wales Conservatory commemorates not only the current holder of the title but also her predecessor, Princess Augusta, who began the gardens in 1759. A wealth of plants is housed in this crystal pyramid.

them. There are three main departments – the Herbarium, the Jodrell Laboratory and the Living Collections.

The Herbarium is where the botanists work (when they are not scouring the globe for new plants) and where a massive collection of pressed and dried plant specimens resides, along with a botanical and horticultural library. It is in here that the world's plants are named and classified. Most folk never get to see this part as it's not open to the general public. Neither are they very concerned with the Jodrell

Laboratory, another private bit, where the plant scientists do their stuff.

Most come to Kew to see what is rather cumbersomely called the Living Collections Division. The plants that grow; they grow as trees in the sylvan glades of the Arboretum, in beds in the Decorative Department, in borders and on rock banks in the Herbaceous and Alpine Department, and in the Temperate and the Tropical Departments they grow under the finest collection of glasshouses in the world. But it was not always so.

On my first day's work at Kew I had to report to the 'T'-Range – a group of greenhouses in the shape of a 'T' which was a part of the Tropical Department. Here grew the giant water lily, *Victoria amazonica*, the carnivorous plants, the

bromeliads and several greenhouses filled with orchids. They were old houses and not in the best state of repair, but the standard of cultivation was high. On my first day I overslept and got a ticking off from Stan Rawlings, the assistant curator. On my second day I overslept again and got a very stern reminder. On the third day I bought an alarm clock. I still have it, and I have my Dip. Hort. (Kew) as well, but Kew no longer has the 'T'-Range. It was eventually demolished and replaced by the simply stunning Princess of Wales Conservatory which was, the guidebook tells you, 'named, by consent of the Queen, in honour of the present Princess of Wales. The Conservatory also recognizes her royal predecessor, Augusta.'

The royal connections do go back a long way. Part of the existing gardens were established by Princess Augusta, who married Frederick, Prince of Wales, in 1736. It was as the Dowager Princess of Wales that she began the garden here in 1759, with William Aiton as her head gardener. Augusta and Frederick's son, who became King George III with Princess Charlotte of Mecklenburg-Strelitz as his Queen, spent much time here, and they appointed Sir Joseph Banks as the unofficial director of the gardens.

Eventually the gardens went through a period of decline and passed from the Crown to the Government in 1840, with Sir William Hooker being appointed the first official director.

Today, Kew is the jewel in the crown of world botany and has also played an important part in history. A Kew gardener looked after the bread-fruit plants that were the cause of the mutiny on the *Bounty*, and Kew introduced rubber trees to Malaya and Ceylon, and cinchona (the source of quinine) to India.

It also introduced me to cockroaches – the 'T'-Range was crawling with them. Pull back a boulder from the side of the giant water lily pool and they would scamper for cover. Go into the mess room at night and turn on the light and they would be all over the walls. I had other encounters with wildlife here, too. If, when topping up the pool, I left the tap running too long the pathway would be awash with floundering guppies, and three or four students could be seen frantically trying to scoop up these little grey fish and get them back in the water.

Surely things are better regulated in the new Princess of Wales Conservatory? As you approach the Conservatory it looks like a series of crystal pyramids rising out of the earth. Enter its portals and you can walk from a dry desert populated by cacti, through temperate areas and tropical rain forests, to a section swamped by ferns of

The giant water lily, Victoria amazonica, *grows in a large pool at the centre of the Princess of Wales Conservatory. First flowered by Joseph Paxton at Chatsworth, it is grown afresh from seed each year and its leaves often measure six feet or more across.*

the mountain foothills where the air is filled with a cool mist that immediately transports you to the Himalayas. All these climates are on different levels so that you climb up into one and down into another. You look down on the pool which houses the giant water lily – its spiny-bottomed, plate-like leaves with their curled up edges are fully six feet across. I have never seen it looking better.

If you enter the Princess of Wales Conservatory in the cactus area you will exit at the end which my old Kew landlady would have called 'Bournemouth'. This replaces a greenhouse that was known simply as 'Number 4', and which was filled with flowering pot plants that would often be found in seaside winter gardens – hence 'Bournemouth'. On the day of my last visit in June it was scented with the perfume of *Lilium regale* and richly banked up with pale pink Canterbury bells.

There is a risk, when you go back to a place twenty years on, that you will find yourself saying 'it's not like it was in my

day'. As far as I'm concerned, that's not the case. I was a student at Kew for three years and then worked as supervisor of staff training for another two years, teaching the gardens staff horticultural skills.

I still know loads of folk who work there, and when I walk around the gardens it's as if I had never left. I do miss having my own key to the garden gate – a huge one with a royal crest on it – and I also miss having my supervisor's bike which would allow me to take off around the three hundred acres whenever I liked.

But now I am happy to tramp – all day if I can find the time – through the green-sward of the Arboretum beneath historic and rare trees, and past the lake with its ornamental waterfowl, enjoying the fact that here every tree and plant is labelled with its name and country of origin and, more often than not, the date on which it was introduced to the gardens.

With this in mind there is one special plant I have to visit today. It grows in the Palm House. This most elegant greenhouse

Nestling among a glade of bluebells in the wilder, woodier part of Kew gardens is Queen Charlotte's Cottage, used as a picnic lodge by the wife of King George III and given to the gardens by Queen Victoria on her Diamond Jubilee.

is the work of architect Decimus Burton and engineer Richard Turner and was built between 1844 and 1848. In 1970 I found myself working inside it for the best part of a year – I was put in charge of the 'cycad end' where a collection of prehistoric palm-like plants grew.

On my first day within its steamy confines I was taken to one particular cycad – *Encephalartos woodii* – and told how to look after it. It grew in a tub four feet high and as much across. 'Don't over water it,' they said, 'it's the only one of its kind in cultivation in the world.' I looked at the date on the label – it had been brought to Kew from Zululand in 1899. My hose-pipe trembled every time I went near that plant, but when I moved into my next department – the Arboretum – it was still alive.

The end of the Princess of Wales Conservatory that houses cool conservatory plants is always colourful because the display is being constantly changed and added to. Lilies scent the air as well as brightening the view.

I have just been to look at it again. It is still clinging on to life though not, I think, in quite as good a condition as when I left it. The fronds are looking a bit yellow at the edges. If I were the student in charge of it now I'd be a mite nervous.

It's impossible to tell you how to walk round Kew as there are so many options. One thing is certain – you'll need at least one full day to do it justice even remotely. It's like taking a botanical tour of the world without ever leaving Surrey and, although ball games and the like are not allowed, there is now much more emphasis on opening the eyes of children to the wonders of Kew. There are huge and informative labels in both the Palm House and the massive Temperate House attached to plants like tea, coffee, cocoa, bananas, cotton and so on, and in the vaults beneath the Palm House there's a wonderful display of tropical fish. What have these to do with gardening? Well, they feed on algae and, as the silver letters on the wall here will tell you, 'without algae there would be no life

on earth – the oceans would be sterile and the land uncolonised'.

Kew is now very conscious of its role in conservation. The guidebook points out that 'the mission of the Royal Botanic Gardens, Kew, is to ensure better management of the Earth's environment by increasing our knowledge and understanding of the plant kingdom: the basis of life on earth'.

But there is no point in banging on about conservation if all you do is bore people to death. To this end the Evolution House (which is inside what used to be the Australian House, behind the Temperate House) has been set up so you can travel in time from primeval mud, three and a half thousand million years ago, through the days when bacteria reigned supreme, then primitive plants like club mosses, horsetails and ferns took over and, finally, the first flowering plant arrived. It is real science fiction stuff – complete with smoke coming out of rocks and a huge waterfall – but this is science fact.

Do make sure you see the wild and woolly bits of Kew as well as the glassy high spots. In the depths of the Arboretum is Queen Charlotte's Cottage – a little thatched picnic lodge used by the wife of King George III and given to the gardens by Queen Victoria on the occasion of her Diamond Jubilee in 1897. This part of the gardens is a picture at bluebell time.

Not too far away is the famous Pagoda, designed by Sir William Chambers and built for Princess Augusta between 1761 and 1762. You can't go up it. In fact it's never been open to the public despite the horror stories of it having to close as too many people threw themselves off the top! Walk around the lake which is in a direct line with the back door of the Palm House – the door that leads into the Rose Garden.

Beyond the lake is the River Thames with Brentford on the opposite bank, but the best view of the river is from the Queen's Garden, laid out around Kew

The Arboretum houses a matchless collection of rare trees and shrubs. In spring, sheets of daffodils spring up below the waxy goblets of Magnolia x soulangeana *before the rest of the trees have come into leaf.*

Palace – a lovely red-brick four-storey dwelling also known as the Dutch House. George III and his family lived here for a while. The Queen's Garden dates from the 1960s when the allotments that preceded it were swept away and a seventeenth-century garden, more in keeping with the palace, was laid out in their stead.

There is a formal parterre, a sunken herb garden surrounded by a laburnum walk and, at the far end, a mound of dwarf box topped by a wrought-iron treillage from which you can see across the river. As a student I was pretty handy with a pair of shears, even though I say it myself, and was asked if I would clip the mound. I was offered the job as overtime, so I have 'the mound' to thank for the fact that I could put down a deposit on my first car.

In fact, so much of my early life as a gardener was tied up with Kew that I still look upon it as my horticultural home.

Yes, a lot has changed, and the garden constabulary look younger than they ever did (some of them are women now), but it is still the Kew where I learned my craft and where I am still welcomed as a member of the Kew Guild and a Life Member of the Kew Students Union.

What I did miss on my latest visit was going in by the staff entrance. I entered, instead, by the Victoria Gate. Now in my day (oops, there, now I've said it) the Victoria Gate was a small turnstile affair by a little wooden hut. It housed a gardens constable whose bike would be leaning up against it as he took your threepenny bit entrance fee.

Today it is the Victoria Gate Visitor's Centre, a swish edifice with lots of plate glass, a smart shop and a shining pool of water skimming under its modern roof supports. It exacts a rather heavier toll than a threepenny bit, but at least it is a grand introduction to a grand garden and plants you in a direct line to the Palm House, which is as good a place as any to begin your tour.

Suggested itinerary? Oh, alright then. Go from the Palm House to the Water Lily House, and then the Princess of Wales Conservatory, and then Kew Palace and the Queen's Garden, passing the Orangery on the way. Then head for the lake, walking round it and passing Queen Charlotte's Cottage and the Pagoda. Stop at the Pavilion Restaurant for refreshments before tackling the Temperate House and the Evolution House. But be warned – there is an abundance of other temptations along the way.

It doesn't matter what time of year you go – height of summer or dead of winter – you'll find there's always something spectacular you have never seen before. And if you're walking quietly down one of the thousands of paths through this botanical paradise and someone passes you on a bicycle, just think to yourself that once upon a time that was me.

The Royal Botanic Gardens, Kew are perhaps the finest botanic gardens in the world and the range of plants they contain is unparalleled. It takes days to work your way through all the delights it has to offer, so rich is the planting.

STICKY WICKET

Dorset

'I'M NOT VERY good with small children and small plants', says Pam Lewis, but from the look of her garden you would never guess. It is a fastidiously-woven counterpane of plants, many of them small, arranged so that their colours blend or complement one another, or contrast cleverly rather than stridently. Nothing jars, no colour combinations offend your eye, and yet the whole place buzzes with vitality.

Peter and Pam Lewis came to Sticky Wicket in 1986 when it was just fields. Two of their three and three-quarters of an acre are still down to pasture, but an acre and a half has been transformed into a garden that sends me scuttling back home with knitted brows. If I plant catmint, lavender and chives and golden marjoram together, will they look as good as this?

You will find their garden in the heart of Dorset, having passed through oddly-named villages like Piddletrenthide and Tolpuddle (the home of the martyrs) and down lanes with high hedge-banks that are awash in May with Queen Anne's lace and red campion, blue-flowered alkanet and Jack-by-the-hedge. Sticky Wicket sits

OPPOSITE *A dense patchwork of herbs and low-growing shrubs, many of them aromatic, carpet the ground in the Round Garden at Sticky Wicket.*

between the church and the school in the village of Buckland Newton, up a lane with a sign saying 'Gaggle of Geese' (the village pub).

The garden surrounds a stone-built bungalow with a conservatory attached. This conservatory acts as a working greenhouse from October to May and a tearoom from June to September when the garden is open one day a week.

It is a couple of weeks before the garden is due to open and Peter and Pam are planting, tidying and gearing up for the

season, which explains why they look a bit shattered. They operate as landscape gardeners, transforming the pocket-handkerchief plots of their clients and, in one case, a more stately eight-acre estate, while attending to their own garden in between times.

'Opening it means that you do have to rally it, but it does get left until last', says

A wicker chair underneath an arbour is the perfect place to sample the fragrances of this Dorset garden.

*Pam Lewis's 'private bed' where her pot
plants and carpeters are woven together in
a pleasing pattern.*

Pam. 'Then, when we've set everybody else
up for the year it's a rush to get it ready.'

I ask if they enjoy opening their garden
to the public.

'It's a chore and a nightmare really.'

So why do they do it?

'At first we did it as a sort of "front
cover". We'd been farming and gardening
before we moved here, and opening the
garden helped us to get the landscaping
business off the ground. Friends suggested
we open it after about two years, and the
response was terrific, so we've kept on.'

Gardening to Pam is an art form;
horticulture is a necessary evil. She doesn't
see herself as a plantswoman, but enjoys
cottage gardening and the art involved in
positioning plants to best effect.

It's time to explore. An apron of gravel
fronts the house and the garden spreads
out from its walls like a full skirt. This is
a country garden surrounded by a small-

holding. Peter and Pam are artful in their
approach to gardening, but never twee.
The garden doesn't look like a magic carpet
plonked down in the middle of Dorset –
its edges blur into the countryside.

It was called Sticky Wicket when they
arrived here, and when they tried walking
across the earth in winter they knew why.
The soil is a good loam, but it overlies clay.

'We imported three or four hundred
tons of gravel and hardcore,' says Peter,
'just so we could get about. But we spent
a minimum on hard landscaping; we stuck
to sleepers and gravel as they were cheap.'

They hand-dug every bed and border
to avoid mixing up what decent loam there
was with the intractable subsoil below.

'But for all that, it's been a witch of a
garden', says Pam.

This is dairy country. The soil is rich,
resulting in lush growth which, at the end
of the season, all too often succumbs to
rust disease, fire-blight, or silver leaf – all
of which they have suffered and recovered
from. Trees have suddenly died after three
or four years and, because the site is windy,

badly drained and in a frost pocket, many
plants have suffered from what Pam calls
'cot deaths'. But you wouldn't have the
faintest inkling of these problems from
looking at the garden.

We turn right outside the front door
and head towards a sign saying 'Frog
Garden'. To both left and right are shrubs
of burnished gold, tinged with red –
Spiraea 'Goldflame' next to *Photinia*
'Red Robin' and a crimson flowered
broom. Wisteria drapes the house wall
behind them. Opposite are domes of
Spiraea 'Gold Mound' with Bowles's
golden rush and cowslips, and you round
the corner to the north-facing part of
the garden where the variegated table
dogwood *Cornus controversa* 'Variegata'
takes pride of place – its flattened branches
carrying serried ranks of cream and green
leaves. Near it is the pool that gives this
part of the garden its name. Frogs, toads
and newts breed here under the branches
of all manner of shrubs and among the toes
of kingcups that wade into the water.

Then you notice the pots by the house
– three of them today – one containing
a white-flowered arum lily, another white
Narcissus 'Sinopel' which Pam considers to
be the best white narcissus (it is delectably
scented), and the third is awash with the
white-flowered form of bleeding heart,
Dicentra spectabilis 'Alba'.

In front of them is a terrace of crisp
gravel peppered with alpines and then,
round the corner to the back of the house,
you meet yet more containers filled with
bold plants – a grey-leafed plectranthus,
a massive angelica, purple lavender, purple
sage and purple parrot tulips. This is a
part of the garden that Pam regards as her
own, as opposed to the most famous patch
where visitors get proprietorial and complain if they don't find their favourite
plants in it year after year.

We walk on in the direction of much
clucking and cock-a-doodle-dooing. There
is no escaping the fact that this is a country

garden – the chicken- and duck-run
encloses a bevy of fowls and two scare-
crows. There are Sebrights, mallard and
snow-geese, and a clattering of wings
overhead turns out to be white doves that,
in a moment of contrived poetry, herald
our approach to the White Garden. This
is not a White Garden in the Sissinghurst
mould, but a wilder White Garden where
plants tumble, frolic and billow out over
the curving grass path that circumnavigates
it. The dovecot is the centre-piece.

Beyond this plump and pallid pillow
of a border is a lush pasture in which
grazes… well, yes, a white horse.

Between the white borders the grass
path leads to the nursery area and a long
polythene tunnel flanked by a vegetable
garden where nasturtiums climb up among
the runner beans. Sweet corn and red-
leafed lettuce jostle with lovage and
strident flowers that are too hot for the
main garden. Above them is the snow-
white blossom of *Malus hupehensis*, a
modest-sized round-headed tree. The
welter of delicately-perfumed flowers that
will be followed by tiny red crab apples,
is an unforgettable sight.

*Foliage and flowers are mixed with an artist's
eye to provide continuity as well as contrast.*

And then we reach the most photo-
graphed part of the garden – the part that
visitors return to see year after year. The
Round Garden is a series of concentric
circular beds. At their centre is a bird-
bath planted in a large round cushion
of camomile. This is the 'monastic garden'
– you can walk round and round and
round it, contemplating, without having
to make any decisions as to where to go.

Here grow catmint, golden marjoram,
lavender, cosmos and other annuals that
are allowed to seed themselves. The colours
are selected so that the rose pinks verge
into the paler pinks and the creams verge
into the yellows. There are mauves and
magentas, blue-purples and violet-purples
with deep crimson behind.

This is a garden for butterflies and bees,
and there are places to sit and take in the
fragrance and the subtle changes of colour.
From the front of the house, where you
now find yourself, the effect is of looking
into a gigantic lustre bowl whose rich
iridescent tones merge together.

You can stand at the centre of this
garden and look up the side of the valley
to a lush green fold, carpeted with emerald
grass, where sheep are sedately mowing the

*The Round Garden, where you can walk in
circles and ponder, without ever having to
worry about where you are going.*

greensward. It is idyllic and, in spite of the
hard work, Peter and Pam are fond of this
'witch of a garden' with the funny name.
At least it means that people remember it,
even if they don't always get the name
quite right. 'Whacky Bottom', one person
called it.

Between June and September you can
admire it yourself, and even at the end of
the season it is not over the hill.

'When we close it in September,' says
Pam, 'I think "poor garden"; it's sort of
playing to an empty auditorium – it wants
to go on because it's still good in a
muddled sort of way. Although I'm
relieved it's all over, I feel a bit sorry that
everything is singing and dancing and no
one's there to enjoy it.'

No one except the chicks, the ducks,
the geese and Clary the white horse, the
butterflies and the bees, the foxes, the
frogs, the toads, the newts and the birds,
the white doves and that mole who keeps
pushing up piles of luscious loam on the
far grass path near the meadow…

HATFIELD HOUSE
Hertfordshire

Now I'm something of a sucker for old houses. Victorian piles I can take or leave, but Georgian and Queen Anne beauties I could gaze at or live in forever. I have no difficulty at all in seeing why Americans go wild over anything more than a couple of hundred years old and I'm sure they would give their back teeth for Hatfield House. It goes back to the reign of Henry VII and has a royal pedigree that puts most other houses (except, perhaps, Hampton Court) in the shade.

It was completed in 1497 for Cardinal Morton, the Bishop of Ely, and part of his Old Palace still stands in the garden. It was here that Henry VIII 'stabled' his children, and here that his daughter learnt that she had become Queen Elizabeth I of England in 1558.

Hatfield House itself dates from 1611 – a Jacobean stately home lived in by the Cecil family and visited by sundry monarchs and notables since its completion. Well, it was only to be expected: William Cecil was Chief Minister to Elizabeth I and his son Robert fulfilled the same office for James I and was made the

1st Earl of Salisbury in 1605. He was also the man who put paid to the Gunpowder Plot. James I visited Hatfield House, so did Charles I, Charles II and Samuel Pepys. Oh, it's had a colourful life.

But for gardeners, one other name is important in Hatfield House's history – that of John Tradescant the Elder. Now all that most gardeners know about Tradescant is the plant named after him – tradescantia. It is a trailer known as 'Wandering Sailor' or 'Wandering Jew'. He deserves a better memorial.

Tradescant was the son of a Suffolk yeoman who went to work as gardener to Robert Cecil in 1610. As jobs went in 1610 this wasn't a bad one. The salary was reasonable and he got to travel and meet people. He was paid £50 a year and was sent all over Europe to bring back new plants, fruits and vegetables to enrich the gardens at Hatfield House. He brought back black mulberries from France (in the hope of promoting English silk weaving) and introduced the Cos lettuce from the Greek island of that name. Subsequent trips yielded vines and roses and he was, without doubt, the driving force behind the stunning garden of French design that appeared at Hatfield.

The original gardens thrived for fifty years or so but then declined and, over the next couple of centuries, they were almost completely swept away. But then came a revival, and John Tradescant's influence can still be felt today, mainly on account of the current Lady Salisbury's passion for the garden. Into it she has worked many of the plants that would have been growing there in Tradescant's time.

What Tradescant would not have known about was Hatfield railway station.

Italian statuary and balustrade ornaments add to the intricacy of the gardens here. The current Marchioness of Salisbury has put her stamp on the planting of beds and borders for continuous pleasure throughout the year.

OPPOSITE *The East Gardens at Hatfield House are delightful with their lollipops of clipped evergreen oak (*Quercus ilex*) which were planted in 1977. They form an avenue down either side of richly planted flowerbeds.*

The Old Palace at Hatfield dates from 1497 and the Knot Garden in front of it from 1984. It is modelled on Elizabethan designs and is furnished with plants that would have been cultivated by John Tradescant the Elder.

It drops you off right outside the main gates of the house where one particular Marquess sits, cast in bronze, with the folds of his majestic robes gathering about his feet, looking grumpily across the road at the station car park. It's an odd sight.

He's overdressed among the Hertfordshire commuters and not exactly thrilled at the prospect of having to look over them for all eternity.

Go past him and up the drive which leads you to the forecourt of the house. Nice change this; I'm used to stately homes that channel cars to some field out of sight of the house. Hatfield has a massive forecourt and it's good to see it used.

There are two main chunks of garden here: the West Gardens and the East

Gardens. The East Gardens are private and only open on Monday afternoons; the West Gardens are for the public and open daily, except Good Friday, from spring to autumn. You must see the East Gardens. No, not just because they are private and I'm a Nosy Parker, but because they represent the most fascinating part of the estate – beautifully laid out and exquisitely planted and maintained.

Looking at the massive north front of the house, the private entrance to the East Gardens is through a hefty wrought-iron gate to the left. It gives access to a terrace that offers a wonderful view down over the lower slopes of this mainly formal garden.

I turn up on a Friday to find the East Gardens closed. What could be done? Would I be able to have a quick look at the private bit? The Colonel was sent for. I mumbled an apology. The Colonel, politeness itself, got on his mobile phone to the head gardener and then ushered me in through the smaller public gate, below the grand one, and asked me if I would mind keeping off the upper terrace which is in full view of the windows of the house. So I was lucky, but please, don't expect to see the East bit on any day except Monday.

This gate enters the Kitchen Garden. Now, in common with most gardeners, I would sell my left leg for a walled kitchen garden, and this one is just such a beauty. Derelict kitchen gardens with crumbling vineries and weed-infested asparagus beds are not hard to find, but it's a real joy to encounter one that's thriving. Here are small raised beds roughly four feet by twelve feet in which grow individual crops – everything from onions and leeks to asparagus and peas, from broad beans and lettuces to 'Primo' cabbages protected by large domes of woven bamboo to keep out the pigeons. I've since been informed that these domes started life as fighting cock baskets from Taiwan!

Large terracotta pots, decorated with the family crest, are home to fig trees and

The Swimming Pool Garden is, not surprisingly, part of the private East Gardens and is surrounded by a tall yew hedge which further adds to its privacy. Standard ornamental trees are dotted about the grass.

citrus fruits, and there are pleached *allées* of apple trees and fruit cages containing currant bushes. Polythene tunnels strike a practical twentieth-century note, as do potatoes growing under the protection of fleece, but there's also a handsome white-painted greenhouse with pelargoniums, agapanthus and electric-blue plumbago.

Rhubarb bursts up from its own well-manured bed, and nearby are Jerusalem artichokes. An archway is furnished with a vine and everywhere there is manure-mulched soil that any self-respecting vegetable would rejoice over. It is the sort of garden that sends many chaps home intent on giving their own vegetables a stiff talking to.

From the Kitchen Garden another gateway leads through to the East Parterre which is a gardener's delight. At either side of it, stretching outwards from the house, are twin avenues of evergreen oaks, *Quercus ilex*. These are not allowed to grow to their usual monstrous proportions,

but are clipped into eight-foot diameter globes like dark green lollipops atop ten-foot-tall trunks. In between these twin avenues, which were only planted in 1977, is a formal pattern of beds edged in dwarf box and packed with all manner of choice border plants and roses. It is a garden with an intimate feel and, below the steps which descend to it from the upper terrace, white fantail pigeons besport themselves around a fountain set

into a niche. It is all rather idyllic, even if the fantails were introduced because of their bullying tactics – they scare off the wood pigeons intent on ripping up the brassicas in the Kitchen Garden.

The peace is shattered suddenly on this June afternoon by the rattle of a hedge trimmer and there, in one corner of the parterre, is a man wearing a strange hat and clipping the box hedges. The hat is a tweed pork-pie type, but around it, sticking out like hunting trophies, are carved wooden heads of a duck, a spaniel, a horse, an owl and other birds and beasts of the country.

The wearer of this headgear of distinction turns out to be Larry Laird, a man who knows a thing or two about hedges, and even more about wood carving. He lays all the hedges on the estate, and elsewhere too, and carves shepherds crooks – but only three a year. Larry has an existence that some would envy; he lives on the estate and never leaves it except to lay

The planting in the box-edged beds of the East Parterre is of great richness. Roses and border perennials – of the sort that complement rather than compete with the blooms of the roses – fill the enclosures to bursting point.

The Maze, which lies below the Swimming Pool Garden, was planted in 1840. During the war it suffered from neglect and then later from outright vandalism; today it is no longer open to the public.

The Herb Garden is situated within the Scented Garden and is centred by a sundial standing on a carpet of chamomile. Old roses and lavender, mixed with fragrant and aromatic herbs, fill the beds and borders on all sides.

hedges. I asked him why he never ventures into the outside world.

'I hate the town', he says. 'I don't want nothing to do with it.'

And where does he live?

'I live in the vineyard; seven acres on the river, with a boat-house. I've been here fifteen years; I used to work on a farm before that, quite a few farms.'

'What a rotten life!', I said.

'Terrible isn't it!', he replied.

The heads on Larry's hat nod up and down in time with his own.

'So is that an advert?', I ask, pointing to the hat.

'No, it's a sculpture in its own right', he says. 'Come and have a look at my crook.'

He leads me to a doorway under the back of the steps where the fantail pigeons are paddling.

'I look after the fantails as well for Lady', he says, nodding his heads in the direction of the cooing and strutting doves.

We walk into the cavernous recess under the steps where he keeps his corn and his tools. It is lofty, lime-washed and vaulted, almost like a wine cellar, lit by a bare bulb. From behind a battered old

chair he pulls out a wooden crook with an ornate top, carved in the form of a reclining lion complete with all kinds of twirly embellishments beneath it.

'It's walnut', he tells me.

I confess to having a few shepherd's crooks myself, but nothing as elaborate as this. Larry says that if I would like him to make me one I will have to get my order in early for next year (he is fully booked for this year). I promise to do so and leave him in the bowels of his steps to continue my tour of the garden.

He'll have his work cut out here, if you will pardon the pun, for below the parterre is a maze of yew. But before this, on the opposite side of the parterre to the Kitchen Garden, is the Mount Garden with two grassy hummocks and a massive chestnut tree between them, circled by a tree seat. Below it is an orchard with cherries, apples and the like growing in buttercup-spattered meadow grass and with a yew-backed arbour at one end, in which nestles a seat. Then there is a grassy ride that leads to the maze. No longer open, thanks to the depredations of assorted juvenile visitors, the view of it from above is worth a look. It

was planted in 1840 and is of an intricate and finely-clipped pattern that can foil the keenest brain. It must cost Larry quite a lot in emery paper to keep his blades sharp enough to tackle this bit of topiary.

Walk past the maze and through the Pool Garden – not one with goldfish but a swimmin pool – surrounded, again, by yew hedges as tall as those of the maze at around eight feet. You are then led further downhill towards the New Pond which is a lake surrounded by meadow grass dotted with young trees and shrubs. The New Pond was created at the same time the house was built (well, everything is relative) and sports Canada geese, black swans, assorted waterfowl and an island. Walk around the pond and admire the views, then retrace your steps and head back towards the house.

I then return to the forecourt. A walk across the north front of the house takes me to the West Gardens on the opposite side, and the first thing I see is a vast horse chestnut, behind which reclines the re-maining wing of the wonderful Old Palace. It is built of a more russety, rufous brick than Hatfield House and, in front of it, is the Knot Garden designed by the present Marchioness and completed in 1981. There are three knots edged by dwarf box, and a foot maze, all arranged around the central fountain. The whole thing is sunk down within daisy-spotted grassy banks. The plants here were all in cultivation during the fifteenth, sixteenth and seventeenth centuries – they would all have been known to John Tradescant the Elder – and you can get a wonderful view of the garden from the raised bank which runs around it on three sides, with the Old Palace on the third. This Knot Garden really is a treasure worth seeing.

Leave it, when you must, by passing under the Lime Walk – a pleached *allée* of green-leafed limes on a rustic framework which runs round the Privy Garden on all four sides. Like the Knot Garden, the larger Privy Garden has a fountain at its centre, and there are beds of border plants and roses all around. It was originally designed by Lady Gwendolen Cecil, youngest daughter of the 3rd Marquess, who was Queen Victoria's Prime Minister. The pattern is much the same today, though some of the materials have changed. It's a jewel box of a garden with beds jam-packed with interesting plants; clumps of this and that placed cheek by jowl so that its appearance changes as spring turns into summer.

Adjacent to the Privy Garden is the Scented Garden with its paved and hoggin path and four-hundred-year-old walls on three sides and a holly hedge on the fourth. The walls, like most of those at Hatfield House, are home to a variety of climbing plants – from wisteria and roses to ceanothus and magnolia. No space is wasted, and no soil is unenriched by crusts

of farmyard manure. No wonder the plants grow well here.

The Scented Garden is a series of rooms – or it will be, when the box hedging surrounding the squares of lawn has grown a little taller. There are 'doorways' linking the different enclosures, and beds and borders are planted up with all manner of fragrant plants and flowers – from the stewed prune aroma of *Ozothamnus ledifolius* to the sweeter scented pinks. This is a living encyclopedia of perfume created from a mixture of border perennials, shrubs and roses. Sniff them, bruise the occasional leaf to release powerful aromas, and catch the rising fruity scent of camo-mile as it is squashed beneath your feet.

In the centre is a sundial surrounded by a herb garden decorated with standard honeysuckles and kerbs of lavender.

Flowers from the Scented Garden are used to make pot-pourri for the house and visitors must surely leave this garden feeling that their nostrils are full to the brim with fragrance.

For that reason, the Wilderness Garden comes as a pleasant change. As you walk

You can escape the formal gardens at Hatfield House with great ease and drift off into the woodland. Even here the ancient trees are being added to with young neighbours to ensure that continuity is achieved over the centuries.

further away from the house mown rides cut through the long grass below tall trees to take you into light woodland peppered with rhododendrons and azaleas and groves of young birch trees.

There is much new planting going on beneath the venerable canopies of ancient trees that will be over the hill in the next century. But that's really the predominant feeling at Hatfield: it's not of a piece of Elizabethan history which has been pickled in aspic, but of a garden into which new life is breathed by the hour. The plantings are in keeping historically, thanks to the painstaking care of Lady Salisbury, but at the same time they are fresh and vibrant, not old and dusty.

I know why the bronze Marquess at the front entrance looks so grumpy – he knows what's behind him, and he's been made to gaze at Hatfield station!

BETH CHATTO GARDENS

Essex

IS GARDENING REALLY a man's game? Have gardening pioneers always been men? There are those who will argue that this is the case, and they will quote the names of gardening luminaries to prove their point: John Claudius Loudon, Joseph Paxton, Graham Stuart Thomas and Christopher Lloyd will spring to their lips. But that is akin to saying that all the great chefs were men. Yes, from Auguste Escoffier to Anton Mosimann there have been men at the handle of the egg whisk, but those who have most influenced domestic cookery have been women: Mrs Beeton, Eliza Acton, Elizabeth David, Jane Grigson and Delia Smith.

Well, the same is true in gardening. Oh, I know that for years it was Mr Middleton or Bill Sowerbutts or Percy Thrower, but they were men whose talents lay in growing plants rather than using them. When it comes to creativity coupled with that craftsmanship, it is women who have

OPPOSITE What was once a marshy hollow is now one of the finest gardens in the country. Lakes have replaced the boggy earth and at the waterside grow arum lilies, bog irises, hostas and other lovers of damp ground.

Linum narbonnense *does not seed readily, so is propagated from cuttings. The problem for Beth Chatto is that demand always exceeds supply.*

most inspired home gardeners: women like Gertrude Jekyll and Vita Sackville-West, Margery Fish and Beth Chatto.

I always think of Beth Chatto as the Elizabeth David of the gardening world, which might be a bit unfair. David was tricky to get on with and that has never been the case with Beth Chatto. She has all the freshness, inventiveness and originality of Elizabeth David, along with a prodigious knowledge of plants (and cookery, funnily enough), but she is never less than great fun to be with.

In gardening circles Beth has become something of a legend in her own lifetime. It was she who turned people's eyes towards out-of-the-ordinary plants back in the 1960s when she opened her 'Unusual Plants' nursery at Elmstead Market. Since then she has inspired thousands of people through her writings – *The Dry Garden* and *The Damp Garden* have become classics – and her exhibits at the Chelsea Flower Show, which have won ten consecutive Gold Medals from the Royal Horticultural Society.

People would make a bee-line for the Chatto exhibit at Chelsea, to ogle the goodies she had brought from her nursery and arranged in a fashion that left many other exhibitors green with envy. It was not just the arrangement of the plants alongside one another which was so breathtaking, it was the fact that they were grouped according to the growing conditions they enjoyed. It is part of the fun of Chelsea Flower Show that you will find rhododendrons and roses, foxgloves and fuchsias, daffodils and chrysanthe-mums, bog irises and rock roses all grouped together – something that could never be possible in 'real life'. But on Beth's

133

On the sun-drenched terraces that slope down from White Barn House, Mediterranean plants do well. The predominant feeling here is of rich planting – low-growing shrubs are interwoven with perennials and bulbs shoot up through the thick rug of foliage.

stand you knew that the combinations were achievable in your own garden – all you needed was the plants and the skill.

Beth no longer exhibits at the Chelsea Flower Show; instead she has her own 'Chelsea' in the fifteen acres that were once part of her husband Andrew's fruit farm at Elmstead Market, near Colchester. It is here that keen gardeners flock like disciples to see the plants growing in varied conditions – from boggy streamside to arid gravel – and where they come to buy from the nursery where hundreds of 'specialist plants' are grown and offered for sale.

I first met Beth about twenty years ago, but it was not until the early 1980s that we became friends and I was taken on my first tour around her garden. My first gardening tips came from my mother

– when I came up to her waist. My last have come from Beth – I come some way above her shoulders!

If you are a keen gardener you will know of the pleasure of garden talk; of the shorthand that exists in conversation: 'Is that repens?', 'Does it set?', 'How long can you keep it?', 'Miffy?', 'Does it run?', that sort of thing. Spending a day with Beth is akin to a second fiddle being allowed to play with a concert violinist. You come away with your own standards elevated.

When I was last there it was early June. After days of dull weather and cloud, the sky, at dawn, was almost clear as I drove down the grizzly A133, Clacton road, turning off after Elmstead Market down the lane signposted 'Beth Chatto Gardens'.

It is a sign of the times, if you will pardon the pun, that 'Unusual Plants' has been replaced by the name of the owner but, since Beth pioneered these rarities in the early 1960s, many others have jumped on the bandwagon and you can now find 'rare and specialist' plant nurseries all over the country. It clearly makes sense

to advertise the name people know, rather than just the concept.

The first surprise is the car park. It is not where it was. A sign funnels me off to the left into a smart enclosure that looks rather like a country racecourse with small paddocks separated by rails. It is only to be expected, I guess, that the tastefulness in garden style should be in evidence even in the car park. But why has it moved? The answer is obvious as I walk towards the gardens through what used to be the car park; it is now a Gravel Garden – awash, if that is not a contradiction in terms, with plants requiring little water and plenty of sun. It is a picture, and proves that over the years the lady has lost none of her touch.

We meet in the office, complain that it has been too long, pick up just where we left off a few years ago with laughs and hugs, and walk out to look at the garden – the gravel garden first. It is barely three years old and already it looks mature.

What was the soil like, I wondered.

'We killed the grass with Round-up and then dug a trench about two feet deep to see what it was like. Well, we've got about four inches of soil and it is just this underneath: gravel and sand – bright yellow – you could have brought your bucket and spade, it was like Frinton!'

So what happened next?

'I put the hose-pipes down to make what looked, I hoped, like a dried-up river bed, with islands and borders. I hope it's worked. One visitor thought it had, she said that "the tide ebbs and flows with the growth of the plants". I thought that was rather nice.'

Beth has never been a paper planner. She plans the shape of her gardens on the soil – always with hose-pipes laid on the earth to mark the lines of beds and borders – and then sets about improving the soil, even here at the top of the garden in the gravel where drought resisters are planted.

The three quarters of an acre of land would not be helped much by rainfall –

this part of Essex enjoys only twenty inches of rain a year, so first the area was tackled with a tractor fitted with a subsoiler to relieve the compaction caused by twenty-five years of car parking. Then the land was ploughed in the autumn and left until January before being rolled and levelled. Garden compost and mushroom compost was added, rotavated in and allowed to settle, and planting began in March. The paths were covered in gravel, but not the beds, which were simply hoed over to remove weeds. Gravel was spread between the plants in their second summer and now many of them have begun seeding themselves in this welcoming protection which keeps their collars dry, prevents mud splashing, helps retain moisture and keeps down weeds.

It would convince anyone to turn at least a part of their plot into a gravel

Beth Chatto is famous for her plant groupings. Not only are the plants situated in order to show one another off to perfection, but they are grown in ground that suits them – be it moisture retentive or dry, sunny or shady.

garden, but here it is a perfect example of Beth's number one dictum: grow plants that suit the prevailing soil and weather conditions. Here in her gravel you will find a rich mixture that really does live up to that over-used gardening term 'patchwork quilt'. There are carpets of anthemis and bergenias perforated by ornamental alliums and *Gladiolus tristis*. Armerias and geraniums, lavenders and poppies are soared over by foxtail lilies (eremurus); rivulets of grey foliage swirl in between welters of green euphorbias or seas of purple sage. The effect is not spotty – it is of bold sweeps of plants with varied colours and textures. There are large, glossy, leathery leaves alongside those that are grey and hairy or light and feathery. Purples contrast with greys or sea greens. Colourful flowers are used only sparingly but nonetheless with great impact.

Many of the plants here are relatively easy to find, thanks to the work of the Chatto nursery, but a few of them are rarities, like the vertical purple-leafed *Phlomis tuberosa* 'Amazone', which towers over its lower-growing neighbours.

'You do need upright shapes,' she says, 'otherwise your plantings end up looking like a tray of scones.' And even in winter the gravel garden has much to offer – the gravel 'gleams and glows', and foliage shows up well against it.

Beth always says that much of her knowledge has come from her husband's study of plants in their habitats, but the placing of plants is her own special talent. As you walk round you will be tempted to scratch down with a pen or a pencil those combinations that are especially stunning.

Beth started life as a teacher and today she still imparts her knowledge with an almost evangelical fervour. Garden visitors come up to say 'hello' and one couple who have come with a son in his late teens ask for an autograph.

'Where are you from?', enquires Beth. 'Ireland, but our son here is in his last

The Gravel Garden was established quite recently on a piece of ground that was previously a car park. The lack of rain in this part of Essex means that drought-loving plants will thrive here.

Down by the side of the lake, in enriched earth well equipped to hold on to moisture, candelabra primulas provide a brilliant spring show, set off by the surrounding foliage of other plants that enjoy the damp soil.

year at Writtle.' Writtle is the local Essex horticultural college.

'Have you been here before?', asks Beth.

'No', says the lad.

'Why not?', asks Beth.

'He hasn't got a car', says his mother, leaping to the lad's defence.

'But haven't the college brought you?'

The youth explains that nowadays the horticultural students spend little time talking about or looking at plants, or discussing the way they grow and their habitats – his course is mainly concerned with business administration and man-management. We both bid farewell to the couple and their lad, saddened by the lack of passion for plants.

But the pall quickly rises as we walk downhill to the place where it all started back in 1960. It was then that Beth and Andrew built the single-storey, split-level, white-painted house on the west-facing bank of the three- or four-acre wilderness that bordered the fruit farm. It was a shallow valley through which ran a spring-fed ditch. Today, thirty-five years on, it is a garden which has acquired a Mediterranean feel on the upper west-facing slopes, in contrast to the shade- and moisture-loving plants which surround the five lakes in the valley bottom.

Always the aim has been to garden with the soil and the environment, rather than against it. In the valley bottom you will find gunneras and lysichitons that would not have a hope in hell of surviving barely fifty yards away on the drier slopes. But soil preparation is everything. Always the earth is enriched with copious amounts of compost, and everywhere it is mulched – either with straw or manure in the centres of beds and borders, or with chipped bark at the front. Moisture, in arid East Anglia, is something to be cherished.

Beth knows that she has been lucky in finding a garden with its own water in this part of the country, but she has achieved this garden by means of hard work, skill with plants, and an undying enthusiasm for everything that grows. She is not a wealthy woman – 'My riches are in the soil', she says – but refuses to let the business grow any larger. Many of her staff have been with her for a long time and are loyal friends, and she wants to feel that she is still a vital part of the business – something she could not do if she said 'yes' to the franchising of her name, rather like a

top couturier whose label can be stitched into the back of any garment. Only, in this case, the branded label would be stuck into a pot and not on to clothes.

To walk around the garden in her company is to see a sharp gardening mind at work. Plant combinations are admired and dissected, errant foxgloves are heaved out, broken in two and left at the side of the bed to be collected later, and plants that have gone over the hill are briefly mourned over and then extracted.

She gets great pleasure from looking up at a tall tree that she has planted, but recognises that the planting below may now have to be adjusted to cope with its elephantine growth.

Before you walk down the slopes into the Water Gardens you will pass the Mediterranean-style Garden where the

Gravel paths snake in serpentine patterns through the Gravel Garden. The earth between the plants is also covered with the small stones, providing ideal conditions for the plants to seed themselves, as well as keeping down weeds and sealing in what little moisture there is.

Mount Etna broom, *Genista aetnensis*, towers over alstroemerias and sedums, cistuses and salvias – the precursor, if you like, of the Gravel Garden. Here are sun-baked beds that positively crackle.

Pots of spiky agaves and aloes decorate the steps down into the valley, and various pots are grouped together and planted up in summer to make miniature gardens of their own with a real Mediterranean feel.

Then, in the valley bottom, are the lakes – man-made by damming the ditch at intervals. Walk the broad, green grassy rides around them and discover that new visions appear at every turn – candelabra primulas and hundreds of juicy hostas reflected in the slow-moving water, huge rare buttercups and ornamental grasses, ferns and irises, all planted to show you just what you can do with plants.

There are living tapestries of purple-leafed violets interwoven with acid-yellow creeping jenny, and banks of spire-forming plants – foxgloves, campanulas and turk's-cap lilies in serried ranks, one behind the other, and all flowering on the same day. In this part of the garden everything seems green and lush, in cool contrast to the dryness of the upper slopes.

Take your camera – there are so many views and the 'gosh' factor is high – and your wallet or cheque book, too. When you have toured the Gravel Garden, the Mediterranean Garden and the Water Gardens in the valley, there is a plant nursery which will have keen gardeners behaving like children in a sweet-shop.

Shelter houses cover the shade lovers and the woodland plants from Adonis to Waldsteinia, and out in the open are the sun-lovers from Acaena to Zauschneria.

I leave with my car boot stuffed with treasures I cannot wait to plant in my own garden – hoping against hope that they will look, in some way, as magical as they do in Beth's garden at White Barn House.

Before I go, she shows me another area of woodland at the far end of the nursery

which is being converted into a woodland garden proper. Here grow the trilliums and the trollius, the ferns and the primulas that love leafy soil and dappled shade. Already much of it has been cleared and planted, and honeysuckles and other climbers are scrambling up the tree trunks. Her girls work at the weeding as we wander through the extra acres that will soon be made a part of the garden.

Why, do you think, at seventy-two, does Beth want to make her garden larger? I do not even bother to ask. It is obvious that the passion is undiminished and that, for her, the greater the challenge, the greater the pleasure.

Above all else, Beth Chatto's garden provides inspiration for those who are keen to position their plants so that they look stunning. This is an artist's garden where contrast in plant shape, texture and colour are used to make tremendous impact. Each year parts of the borders are 'unpicked' so that a new tapestry of plants can be stitched into them.

'Don't you feel daunted by it all?', I enquire.

'Oh, yes', she says. 'When I told Graham Thomas that I was going to turn this bit of wood into a woodland garden he said "Beth, I beg of you, don't do it!" But I have. And it's going to be lovely.'

HOLKER HALL
Cumbria

THE HOTEL IS in Grange-over-Sands and its windows look out across the wide expanse of Morecambe Bay which, on this Midsummer Night, appears as dry and seemingly as large as the Sahara Desert.

In the evening I sit out on the hotel terrace, with a pint of local bitter and a plate of local fish, until the sun goes down putting the power station in the shadows. Why am I telling you all this? Well, I just like to get you in the mood.

In the morning I set off for Holker Hall, the home of Lord and Lady Cavendish. It's been their family home since 1756. Today it's famed not only for its gardens, but also for the annual Great Garden and Countryside Festival, held each year during the first week in June.

I had heard that the name of the house was not pronounced phonetically and so thought it best to enquire of the two girls at reception. The first, with a delicious Lancashire accent, said: 'Oh; it's called Holkerr Hall.' The second girl raised her eyebrows: 'I think Lady Cavendish would like you to pronounce it "Hooker".' I made a mental note that should I meet

OPPOSITE *The Rose Garden at Holker Hall is stuffed with old-fashioned roses that scent the air in late June and early July. Originally laid out by Thomas Mawson, it has since been redesigned and replanted.*

Twin gazebos provide somewhere pleasant to sit in the Rose Garden. There are views across green lawns back towards the house, or into the centre of the garden where an Italian lion's head dribbles water into a rectangular pool.

Lady Cavendish, I would make sure I was with the 'Hookers'.

The drive to Holker Hall takes around fifteen minutes from Grange, passing through Dickensian-sounding villages like Allithwaite, Flookburgh and, eventually, Cark-in-Cartmel where you will find Holker Hall itself. Through large stone pillars you pass, and on past the obligatory little hut, though here it is four-square and grey-pillared against a white background, with a little orb at each corner of its flat roof – an aristocratic hut.

You'll continue through rolling parkland with the venerable oaks one expects around a stately home and you'll eventually arrive at the car park, near the shop and the clock-topped stable yard tearooms. You can then walk downhill and underneath the sweeping branches of a huge beech tree to the white wrought-iron garden gate which nestles at the side of Holker Hall, a wondrous pinkish-grey Victorian pile that was built to replace much of the previous house after a disastrous fire in 1871.

The part of the garden you enter first is a formal delight; a modern formal delight perhaps fifty yards square. Until recently it was dominated by rather oppressive yews, but under the influence of Grania, Lady Cavendish, it has been completely renovated and turned into a garden of great vibrancy. There are climbers on the pink stone walls of the house – sun-loving ceanothus, *Solanum crispum* and white-flowered *Abutilon vitifolium* – and, to lead you into the formal part of the garden with its elliptical central area, are sweet peas trained up trellis obelisks.

The beds here are simply stuffed with perennials – great foaming mounds of lavenders and rosemary, catmint running upright through pea-sticks among delphiniums and peonies, irises and crambe, sages and pyrethrums, roses and buddleias. On one side of this garden is a

Throughout the gardens at Holker Hall there are mature trees and vast domes of rhododendrons. Some of the trees date back two hundred years to the time of Lord George Cavendish; many more were planted during the nineteenth century.

border about eight feet wide in which are planted sweet peas – not up supports, but as ground cover, running over the enriched earth below a tunnel of espalier apple trees. The feeling is not of an ancient stately garden preserved for posterity, but of an exciting new development that still manages to complement the old blushing house.

Round the back of the house are beds of pot marigolds surrounded by lady's mantle, and a daisy-dotted croquet lawn – the only part of the garden marked private, the rest is liberty hall. The yew hedges are speckled with the scarlet tubular blooms of the flame creeper, *Tropaeolum speciosum*.

From the new Formal Garden the pathway leads down steps to another formal area – this time long and rectangular, where the central walkway is covered by a tunnel of pleached Portuguese laurel (*Prunus lusitanica*). Here you'll find lollipop-trained silver-leaf pears (*Pyrus salicifolia* 'Pendula') whose twisted silver

and white leaves lend themselves well to this butchery. The beds in which they grow are packed with ornamental-leafed kale – much more fun than begonias.

Crataegus trees in square beds are underplanted with annual echiums and the whole garden – whose pastel pink and pale blue scheme is occasionally enlivened by a bright splash of orange – is surrounded by a tall beech hedge.

An archway beckons you through the hedge at the bottom of these Summer Gardens, as they are called, and suddenly you are in a wild flower meadow backed by the Lakeland fells, where mown rides weave in and out of buttercups that push up among the pale lilac haze of the flowering hay. Swallows skim the hayfield catching midges as you walk towards the iron kissing-gate in the direction of what seems like a black satellite dish perched, resembling a giant saucer, on top of a flat rock in the middle of the cow pasture.

It's a sundial; the shadow of its central spike shows the time against the gilded numerals that are engraved into its blue-grey slate face.

Retrace your steps and then, beckoned by two obelisks on your left, re-enter the garden and walk towards the fountain,

whose dish shape seems to mirror that of the satellite-dish sundial.

On reaching it the ground rises and you can enjoy another new feature of Holker. This is the Cascade, a more modest but equally enjoyable version of a feature in the garden of Chatsworth (owned by another branch of the Cavendish family). Inspired by an ancient water garden in Rajasthan, India, visited by the family in 1989, its steps rise towards a statue of Neptune on the brow of the hill in front of you. On either side of the steps are rills whose water tumbles downhill over cobbles and herring-bone slates. The Cavendish snake is set in a mosaic pattern under your feet, along with the figure of a porcupine, and when the rills reach the bottom of the steps their water disappears underground down spiral helter-skelters.

Borders of hostas and ferns flank the rill on its shady passage through the trees, and at the top you'll see close-mown grassy banks that fall away towards the Rose Garden. All around are mighty trees in seemingly infinite variety and elephantine domes of rhododendrons that make this garden a picture in spring.

The Cascade is a new feature, built since 1988. Water tumbles down twin rills at either side of a staircase that climbs upwards to a marble statue of Neptune. Hostas and ferns are planted in the shady earth beneath the trees.

It's a mild garden – thanks to the effects of the Gulf Stream – and seldom suffers severe frosts. The soil is acid and well suited to lime haters like rhododendrons, azaleas and camellias.

Today I spot, when wandering through the grounds, great flame-licked specimens of the Chilean fire bush, *Embothrium coccineum*, simply lighting up the shrubberies with their scarlet tubular flowers. They're a rare and grand sight.

There are some lovely surprises – like the see-saw beneath a giant sycamore. And the swing. At first, all I can see is a girl swinging slowly to right and left like the girl in the Fragonard painting, but instead of pink silk and layers of white petticoat were baggy shorts and a white shirt.

The great thing about the twenty-five acres of pleasure gardens at Holker Hall is that they seem to marry past with future. The earliest records show that in 1720 the gardens were formal, with much topiary and statuary. Between 1783 and 1793 Lord George Augustus Cavendish (godson of George II and Comptroller of the Royal Household) made his own mark on the gardens by sweeping away the formality and going in for the 'natural landscape', in keeping with the fashion of the times. The huge Cedar of Lebanon dates from that time, and today you will also find trees at Holker that were introduced by the 7th Duke of Devonshire, who spent much time here and took advantage of the advice given to him by Joseph Paxton, who was Head Gardener to the 6th Duke.

The Rose Garden was originally designed for Lady Moyra Cavendish by Thomas Mawson, a landscape architect and gardener who ran the Lakeland Nurseries in Windermere in the early part of the 1900s. Now it's been almost completely redesigned, but you come upon it, rather like an oasis, when walking through the less formal part of the garden.

A raised walkway at the back of the Rose Garden has a pigeon house at one

end and a shady summerhouse at the other, edged by a stone pool whose lion head spurts water to send the calm surface into endless ripples. The tall stone wall behind it is capped by plump-breasted pigeons, cooing for all they are worth, and festooned with fragrant roses, clematis, jasmine and abutilon. The beds down below are a welter of old-fashioned shrub roses, underplanted with rosemary, lavender, catmint, pinks and lady's mantle. I walk among them in the sun, drinking in the perfume of dozens of different varieties, and sit down to rest in one of the twin trellis-work gazebos that are almost suffocated by the surrounding blooms. At the foot of the steps that lead down from the raised walkway a motto is carved into the stone:

Here shall ye see no enemy but winter and rough weather.

The garden at Holker today owes much to the enthusiasm of Lord Cavendish, with his sense of family history and continuity, and Lady Cavendish, with her eye for design and planting. I come across her when I return to the formal garden. Well, actually, I come across her dog first – a

The Formal Garden next to the Hall itself is quite new and the planting extremely lavish. Within formal lines are great banks of roses and perennials, sweet peas grown as ground cover and a tunnel of espalier apple trees.

gentle lurcher bitch who plonks herself at my feet as I sit on a bench in the midday sun. And then I see the dog's mistress, at the handles of a cart filled with plants. She's lifting them out and putting them where they are to be planted. The visitors walk around her, as you would around a gardener absorbed in the exacting task of planting up a flower-bed. It would seem rude to interrupt.

Perhaps I'll say 'hello' after all. But before I can move the lurcher is up and across the path barking away at a golden labrador which is acting as a guide-dog. The two animals – one protecting its territory and the other its partially-sighted owner – are separated with polite diplomacy. The moment has gone. And so has her ladyship – back into Holker Hall. Hey-ho. Not to worry. And anyway, in the heat of the moment – and of the afternoon – I would most likely have said 'Holkerr' and not 'Hooker'.

BIDDULPH GRANGE

Staffordshire

YOU WOULD THINK in a book entitled *Favourite Gardens* that every garden mentioned would be a favourite, and this would not be an unreasonable assumption. So I am sorry to have to surprise you and say that Biddulph Grange is not one of my favourites! Now, before you think I am one sandwich short of a picnic, I had better explain why it is here. It is here because I have never seen anything quite as outrageous. You see, it is such an oddity. There is no other garden quite like it, and it bridges the gap between those natural-looking 'Capability' Brown landscapes of the eighteenth century and the plant-filled and intricately-designed gardens of the twentieth century. Not that it is a boring history lesson, far from it, Biddulph Grange is positively lurid.

The early nineteenth century saw a kind of revolt against Brown's trees, lakes and pastures – all of them constructed with

OPPOSITE The garden known as 'China' was a wreck before its restoration in 1988. Now it is resplendent in its original brilliant colours. A willow-pattern bridge crosses the pool in front of a Chinese temple whose eaves are hung with little brass bells.

a limited number of mainly native plants. The landscape architect, Humphry Repton, followed on from Brown and did, at least, have the grace to include a wider range of plants and flowering shrubs which Brown would have tucked away somewhere in a walled garden.

But the early Victorian era saw an explosion in plant collecting overseas. When all these exotic goodies were brought back to Blighty the patrons of the expeditions and other keen gardeners who could lay their hands on such booty naturally wanted to show off their plunder. There was no way they were going to tuck such treasures away behind a wall – they needed to create a garden environment that would show them off to best effect – and so the 'gardenesque' movement, in which the plants were as important as their setting, was born. And so, with the prolific gardening writer John Claudius Loudon at its helm, the Victorian era saw a change in gardening style. Mind you, Loudon was not a fan of the fussy and the over ornamented, and it would have been amusing to hear what he thought about Biddulph Grange. It will be amusing to see what you make of it, too.

A full-size gilded water buffalo reclines under a lacquered canopy on top of a wall and dragons decorate the ground beneath it. This part of the garden could never be accused of subtlety.

The road between Congleton and Stoke-on-Trent does not look terribly promising in gardening terms, but a signposted turning leads you up a drive to a car park from where you can walk towards a vast Victorian house of sootied stone which once belonged to the Bateman family. James and Maria Bateman lived here from 1840 to 1868. He was an orchid enthusiast and she had a passion for lilies and herbaceous plants. Together with their friend, the marine painter Edward Cooke, they created a garden of incomparable Victorian intricacy which has recently been restored by The National Trust. Do not be surprised to find yourself saying 'good heavens' or 'gosh' quite a lot.

You will enter the garden through the house, much of it rebuilt after a disastrous fire of 1896, though the soot-encrusted urns that decorate the rooftops still show the effects of the conflagration. French windows lead you to a double flight of steps that descends into the Italian Garden – twin borders planted up with rather nasty scarlet salvias, African marigolds and lobelia – and eventually leads you to a yew-filled circle at the end. So the start of the journey is a bit disappointing.

Beneath the house are several terraces, like this one, formally planted up with monkey-puzzle trees. Beyond the balustrade is a lake, bordered by huge mounds of rhododendrons, whose surface is speckled with water-lily pads.

A small formal garden with monkey puzzles and yew appears to your left and then, far more spectacular is the Dahlia Walk, which is now almost the entire length of the house. Great banks of dahlias billow out up the slopes where once huge buttresses of yew provided separating balustrades between the different varieties. The Dahlia Walk disappeared when the house became a hospital back in the 1920s, but it was rediscovered, excavated and replanted in 1988, yews and all. Above it the long, cream-painted and peeling hospital extension to the house sits like some brooding sanatorium. I wonder if they'll knock it down?

At the end of the Dahlia Walk you're in for your first treat: your first experience of the Biddulph Time Machine. Enter the pink sandstone Shelter House by its arch-way and then turn right. Almost as if you were in a scene from *The Lion, the Witch and the Wardrobe* you'll suddenly find yourself on a stepped pathway flanked by heaps of old tree stumps arranged in an intricate three-dimensional jig-saw. 'This', says the little old lady who sees my baffled

Biddulph Grange itself is a massive Victorian pile, rebuilt after being all but destroyed by fire in 1896. James and Maria Bateman created the garden between 1840 and 1868, along with their friend Edward Cooke.

expression, 'is the Stumpery.' And she's right. Yews hover above them and ferns spring up among the rotting, moss-covered wood in the shaded, leafy soil. This is a Victorian speciality – some of the original stumps have been replaced, but others have survived. Already you've journeyed back in time. But prepare yourself; you are about to travel east. Turn right at the end of the Stumpery and you are in China.

The up-and-down stone paths lead you into a secluded area which is surrounded by high banks, sections of stone wall (the 'Great Wall of China') and vast trees – sequoias and maples, Japanese cedar and paulownias. In front of you is a scene straight from the willow-pattern plate, except that the woodwork is painted in red, yellow and green, not in that wonder-ful shade of blue.

This garden was a crumbling wreck until restoration work began in 1988, and now 'China' is seen as it would have been in its Victorian hey-day – brightly-coloured lacquer and all.

A willow-pattern bridge crosses a pool which is flanked by maples, bamboos and ferns. Beyond the pool is an intricately-fretworked Chinese temple whose eaves are decorated with little brass bells. Gilded dragons holding bells in their mouths perch on the four corners of the temple roof. Behind you on a knoll amid the trees is a Joss House in similar livery. Here in this Oriental dell grow plants brought back from China – maples, tree peonies, rhododendrons and azaleas – that left Victorian gardeners wide-eyed in amazement.

The gilded Water Buffalo sitting on the wall to the right of the Temple had the same effect on me. Is it real gold leaf on this life-size reclining bovine? It sits under its own lacquered canopy like some prize item of Smithfield livestock, and below it are red gravel dragons set into the grass. Enough, enough, time to move on. Hurry past the gigantic stone frog and make your exit through the Temple.

The Temple leads to a stone cave which turns into a tunnel – the sort that, in Tibet, would probably bring you out in Shangri-La. Instead, it brings you to the huge rocky monoliths of the Glen where the Batemans grew rhododendrons from Bhutan and Sikkim. Most of them died out, but today they are being re-introduced, as are ferns which thrive in the shady crevices among the monstrous boulders. The feeling here is a welcome cool-down from the ornate fussiness of China, and if you journey on with the twists of the path it will take you round a delightfully informal lily pool whose surface is skimmed by huge carp. There are banks of rhododendrons around you, and eventually you are back at the Italian Garden.

But there are delights and countries yet to be visited. Retrace your steps a little, go under a tunnel and follow a long, curving path that takes you through the Pinetum. Here are towering pines, cedars and monkey-puzzle trees with heathers planted in the ground below. It's a walk that will

cleanse the palate for the next culture shock. At the end of the path you will come to the Cheshire Cottage. It's like a rather grand doll's house with a half-timbered front painted in maroon and cream. At either side of the leaded lights above the entrance is the date '1856', and the Batemans' initials are also worked into the timber.

But when you enter the cottage you are no longer in Cheshire, but Egypt. In the sinister rosy glow of red light bulbs squats a beast called the Ape of Thoth and, as you rise out of the tomb-like interior, you will find yourself confronted by Egyptian sphinxes and a gigantic pyramid of yew flanked by yew obelisks. It's all very unsettling. Are you in Staffordshire or Cairo?

But no, it must be Britain, for here, outside 'Egypt', are three very English gardens – the Cherry Orchard Garden, a garden filled with miniature and patio roses, and Mrs Bateman's Garden planted up with verbena.

Look below and you find yourself on terraces above the Dahlia Walk. How does it all fit together? Climb to the upper storey of the Shelter House at the end of the Dahlia Walk and you will have a better view of the garden, as well as the moors beyond, but you will be no nearer to

The Pinetum at Biddulph Grange offers a welcome respite from the elaborate ornamentation in other parts of the garden. Here the atmosphere is cool and beneath the tall trees – coniferous and deciduous – rhododendrons thrive.

discovering just what made James and Maria Bateman spend all their money on creating such an amazing garden.

The cost became prohibitive in the late 1860s and Bateman's son eventually sold the house in 1871. The Batemans retired to Worthing where Maria died in 1895 and James in 1897. The fire of 1896 destroyed much of the house, which was then owned by a Staffordshire industrialist, but it was restored before becoming a hospital in the 1920s. Gradually the garden fell into disrepair; there are pictures of its temples and bridges in a very sorry state, but its acquisition by The National Trust has assured it of a colourful future. As colourful as those Victorian gardeners would have liked it to be.

Biddulph Grange is a great place to visit with the family – children could well be converted to gardening by exploring the place. Me? I am happy to have been there and seen it, but I would not want to own it. Know what I mean?

CRATHES CASTLE

Grampian

'THE BURNETTS WERE not necessarily the most ambitious or violent of families, but they were men and women of culture and warmth', says the Crathes Castle guidebook. To the inhabitants of Banchory, where the Burnetts occupied the local castle for more than 350 years, that must have come as something of a relief. But they were a colourful bunch – a family that included the smattering of admirals and generals, judges and bishops that you would expect from the Scottish nobility, but also a few black sheep and a Governor of New York. Why he wanted to leave I don't know; after all Crathes Castle is in a wonderful setting by the River Dee. He obviously wasn't a fisherman.

The estate came to the Burnett, or Burnard, family in 1308 – granted to them by Robert the Bruce. The hunting horn known as 'The Horn of Leys', which was reputedly presented to Alexander Burnard by Robert the Bruce in 1323, still hangs in the Castle.

The Castle itself dates from 1596 and today it stands as solid as ever in one corner of a series of superb gardens. On a sunny day, against a blue sky, it is blush pink; when the weather is foul it becomes a

mixture of ochre and grey, resolute against the biting winds.

The gardens were created in the 1920s – the work of Sir James and Lady Sybil Burnett – and along with the Castle they remained in the family until 1951, when they were handed over to The National Trust for Scotland by Sir Alexander William Burnett Ramsay, who had taken up residence in Australia – warmer, but not nearly so imposing.

Approaching Crathes Castle through the woodlands of Royal Deeside, I pass a lake to the right, and then wind up the hill to the Castle gates. It looks like a castle should look – tall and impressive, with little round towers at the corners, each with a cone-shaped roof. There is a weathercock and a gilt-faced clock and the family's standard flutters in the stiff Scottish breeze. Water spouts jut out from below the corner towers like small canons.

Castles like this were built to last – the walls at the base are five feet thick – and the rough-hewn granite that was used in the building was rendered with harling for improved weatherproofing. This is a *château* par excellence.

The Walled Garden at Crathes is a gem and the tall stone walls may well be as old as the Castle itself. Within them are eight distinct areas, each with different names and offering different moods and

The granite dovecot, known here as 'The Doocot', is positioned in the farthest corner of the garden, where it was built in 1937.

effects. They are dominated by several tall yew hedges and chunks of yew topiary which have become something of a Crathes trademark.

Sir James and Lady Sybil Burnett were a perfect couple as far as gardening goes. He was a tree and shrub man, a friend of Sir Harold Hillier (of the famous Winchester nurseries), and she was a lover of border perennials and a fan of Gertrude Jekyll. Back in 1895 Jekyll had visited the

OPPOSITE *Granite built and dating from the sixteenth century, Crathes Castle commands fine views over the gardens that surround it.*

The monstrous yew hedges at Crathes have had plenty of time to put on weight – they were planted in 1702.

garden when it was under the care of Sir Robert Burnett and, by all accounts, was impressed not only with the 'brilliancy of the colour masses', but also by the size of the gooseberries. I never thought of Gertrude Jekyll as a gooseberry fancier. Life is full of surprises.

The area within the walls amounts to three and three-quarter acres of neutral to slightly acid loam, and the yew hedges and borders act as divisions between the different areas. Four of the gardens are on a higher level, but you enter on the lower level, from where the view is delightful.

I am gazing down a pathway between borders stuffed with white-flowered plants. The White Borders, with their varied selection of perennials and shrubs, are a treat in early summer when the orange-blossom-scented flowers of philadelphus intoxicate the air above the welter of perennials below. The focal point of the view straight ahead is something I always think of when Crathes is mentioned. It is nothing particularly rare or choice, but it just seems to fit its situation perfectly. A tall, broad, tightly clipped dome of Portugal laurel stands, like an evergreen parasol, half way down the White Borders, where they are criss-crossed by another path which is flanked by shrub and herbaceous borders which look good from June until October.

The laurel acts as a hub or a roundabout on which the borders pivot. If you look into the borders you'll discover a nifty method of staking. It's an idea I pinched and used in my own garden, having seen it at Crathes, and it works well. Stout dahlia stakes are knocked in at six feet intervals along the back of the border, and at similar intervals a couple of feet behind the front of the border. When hammered in they should protrude for a couple of feet. In early spring, just as the plants are beginning to grow, 4-inch wide plastic mesh (of the kind sold to support runner beans) is stretched horizontally across the stakes and secured to them. As the plants grow they push up through the netting which then supports them, invisibly. The netting is covered by foliage, so you don't have to look at it, and yet it stops the plants from flopping. Lower-growing plants at the front of the border will mask the front edge. A neat trick, eh?

The planting at Crathes is not all pastel-shaded and muted; there are areas where, in late summer, brilliant orange and scarlet dahlias create a startling show, and where the rich purples, blues and reds of the lupins, irises and pyrethrums in the June Border lead the eye to another unique Crathes feature – the Doocot – set in a corner of the lower garden. This granite-built dovecot has been on this site only since 1937, but looks perfectly at home, flanked by evergreens and climbers and fitted with an apron of glossy-leafed bergenias. Its roof has the feel of a pagoda about it and when I visited the garden there were great mounds of *Rosa gallica* 'Versicolor', better known as 'Rosa Mundi', billowing out below it, the pink and white candy-striped flowers a-hum with bees.

If you are here in July, go and look at the nursery area below the Doocot to see the amazing spires of the giant lily, *Cardiocrinum giganteum*, whose white, purple-stained trumpets hang from broomhandle-thick stems that are eight feet tall. The cool, moist atmosphere of this part of Scotland, along with the leafy, organic soil, suits them down to the ground (or up to the sky) and they have a delectable scent.

You'll notice amazing growth on other plants at Crathes. Take the magenta-flowered and black-eyed *Geranium psilostemon*. In my Hampshire garden it reaches a comfortable four feet. Up here it makes mounds fully seven feet tall between which you can walk and lose yourself.

Many of the smaller gardens within the larger garden are colour themed – the Red Garden and the Golden Garden, for instance – but there are other, unnamed parts that will delight you. The wrought-iron gate that passes from the Walled Garden into the Wild Garden has clouds of blue catmint at either side. The scent on a warm summer's day is unforgettable – and not just to cats.

The old greenhouses at Crathes act as the dividing line between the upper and lower parts of the garden, and they face south with their backs very firmly to a stout wall, rising in five sections as they climb the slope. Within them are pelargoniums and fuchsias, Malmaison carnations and other flowering pot plants, while the borders outside, filled with half-hardy annuals and tender perennials, are edged with tiny kerbs of box. It's ages since I first visited the garden here, but I remember coveting these modest but delightful three-quarter span greenhouses even then.

To the side of the greenhouses is the entrance to the upper level of the garden, where the great bolsters and finials of yew sit to one side of the croquet lawn (which has been used for this fiercely competitive sport ever since it became fashionable, more than a century ago). Above, to the left, is the Castle, and across the lawn, directly below it, is the Colour Garden or Upper Pool Garden, a heady mixture of purple-leafed Smoke bush, *Cotinus coggygria* 'Royal Purple', Yellow-leafed elder, *Sambucus racemosa* 'Plumosa Aurea', and flowers in strident tones. Reds, yellows and bronzes predominate and a pool with clipped yews at its four corners forms the centre-piece.

The famous Crathes yews make a great screen which divides the upper level of the walled garden in half. Planted in 1702, they are equipped with crisply-clipped orbs as ornamentation and decorated in summer with the brilliant red Flame creeper, *Tropaeolum speciosum*.

Plants have to be tough to survive up here, but those that do weather the storms can give those south of the border a good run for their money.

And the black sheep of the family? Ah, that was young Alexander Burnett, who died in 1648 having been a 'dissolute and naughty student', and who managed to father six children before the age of twenty-six. Like many family members, his was far from being a dull life.

So when you visit Crathes, look up at the pink stone of the Castle and pause for a moment to muse upon its past – every bit as colourful as the garden. ❦

Many of the border plants at Crathes are provided with invisible support in the form of horizontal plastic netting.

Focal points are a feature at Crathes – whether they be in the form of topiary, dovecots or well-placed urns like this one in the Red Garden.

TRESCO ABBEY

Isles of Scilly

EVERY NOW AND then – and not as frequently as you would like – life takes you by surprise and you enjoy what could be described as the perfect day. You can't plan it – it just happens; often when you least expect it. My visit to the island of Tresco was a day like this.

I made the ten-minute car journey from my hotel in Mousehole to Penzance, parked, bought my ticket and boarded the small white ship with the yellow funnel. Not for me the shorter helicopter trip which some visitors take. At 9.15am precisely, the ship the locals call 'The Great White Stomach Pump' set sail for the Isles of Scilly with at least one passenger hoping she would not live up to her name.

The *Scillonian III* rolled a little, but nothing too terrible, and I could feel my face turning brown in the sea breeze. A couple of boats with full sails creamed past us with their orange-coated crews leaning out over the sides. The Cornish coast faded from view. The sky was the colour of forget-me-nots; the sea was blue-black ink.

An hour and a half after leaving Penzance, a faint shadow of islands

appeared on the horizon, and two hours later we cruised past St Agnes, with its green slopes and white lighthouse, and into the harbour at St Mary's.

The passengers toddled off into Hugh Town, the community that cradles the harbour, except for those of us who were bound on our second voyage. We scrambled down the stone steps of the jetty and into the bright red launch *Sea King* – around fifty of us, I guess, seated down the sides and across the middle of the elderly open-topped wooden boat. It left the harbour and bobbed out towards Tresco, an island two miles long and one mile wide whose white sandy beaches really do look like those of the Caribbean and whose water is a rich blue-green.

St Martin's and the Eastern Isles are over to starboard, rocky at the edges and green above, and Tresco is straight ahead, with Bryher and Samson to port. Lovely names. There are 150 islets here; only five of them inhabited. We nudged our way alongside a tiny stone jetty at Carn Near and the passengers began the half-mile walk up the slipway to the famous Tresco Abbey Gardens.

I sit on the rocks by the jetty for a while, watching *Sea King* bobbing back over to St Mary's. The crowd has gone and the day is fine and fair. Razorbills skim low over the water in groups of half a dozen,

and the breeze rustles through the heather and reeds behind me. There are no cars on the island, only a van or two and some tractors, so there is no sound, except for the slap of the tide against the jetty and the call of seabirds.

I set off in the midday sun up the narrow concrete road, often overblown by soft white sand, among the bracken, the heather, the figwort and the campions, and occasional clumps of red-hot pokers and agapanthus.

Every drystone wall erupts with succulents that can eke out a living on dry dust.

A wall clothed with the rosettes of aeoniums and the bright daisies of lampranthus is topped by a spiky Dasylirion acrotrichum.

monks, and successive generations of the Dorrien-Smith family have continued to enlarge and improve the wondrous garden that surrounds it.

Today it is Robert Dorrien-Smith and his family who preside over this incomparable garden, and in case you think they have it cushy in this part of the world, it is as well to remember the events of 1987 and 1990. In January 1987 the garden was hit by the hardest weather the Scillies had ever experienced. Temperatures plummeted, snow fell, and between seventy and eighty per cent of the plants were killed. The scene was heart-breaking, but replanting began immediately.

In the winter of 1990 came another blow – severe gales ripped down the windbreaks, 800 large trees went in one night. The plants that had not been killed by the snowfall perished in the teeth of the gale – acacias and eucalyptus, *Cupressus macrocarpa*, *Pinus radiata* and *Quercus ilex* tumbled into heaps. Over the last few years the job of putting back these windbreaks has been the number one priority, but elsewhere in the gardens you would not know anything had happened. The Phoenix of Tresco has risen from the ashes and become, once more, the most remarkable garden of its kind in the country.

You walk down a path flanked by massive pale blue candlesticks of *Echium pininana*, up to fifteen feet tall, and then between giant gunnera plants and Cabbage palms, finally entering the gardens and heading, if it is lunchtime, for the café. It was, and I did, only to be whisked out of the queue by the curator, Mike Nelhams, with a 'What are you doing here? Come to the hotel for lunch.'

Mike Nelhams has, he admits, the finest gardening job in the world. He is in charge of a patch of paradise, he goes up to

And then a corner is rounded, the ground levels off into an airstrip and helicopter landing pad, and across it is Tresco Abbey itself, surrounded by a drystone wall that is hung with colourful rugs of pink, mauve, purple and magenta lampranthus and studded with the fleshy rosettes of aeoniums. White-painted lean-to greenhouses rise up behind it.

The bright daisies are the first indication that this is no ordinary part of the British Isles. It is washed by that warm breath of air known as the Gulf Stream.

Thirty inches of rain fall each year, mainly between October and March. The temperature seldom falls below 5 or 6°C in winter, and for 350 days is at least 10°C, which means that a wide range of Mexican and Australian plants will thrive.

It is a fact that was discovered in 1834, when Augustus Smith took a leasehold on all the islands as Lord Proprietor and decided that Tresco was the one on which he would live. He built his house, Tresco Abbey, on the site of the ruined abbey of St Nicholas, once lived in by Benedictine

London every now and then to judge at the Royal Horticultural Society's flower shows, and he escorts the occasional cruise around the Mediterranean, where the flora is similar to that on Tresco but not as wide ranging. It's strange to think that the South of France does not possess a climate suitable for some of the plants that thrive on Tresco – the fact that the lower slopes of the garden are slightly more humid means that New Zealand plants do well here, too.

To tour the garden with Mike is a treat. He bursts with enthusiasm for his plants – be they towering furcraeas with pendulous candelabra of pale green blooms or the New Zealand Flame trees (*Metrosideros robusta*) – red-flowered giants that are now regenerating following their drastic pruning after the gale.

The garden pivots around the central Lighthouse Path which looks right up the slope of the island towards a figurehead of King Neptune. Climb this path, past the enormous hedges of evergreen oak almost thirty feet high, and look down. You gaze over the tops of palm trees to the craggy headland and the sea beyond. Subsequent

An American agave, nestling among other sun lovers, is on the point of sending up its spectacular flower spike.

paths come off this central one at right angles, each leading you to a part of the garden that has a different feel. There is a terrace effect here; the middle of the garden is very much Mediterranean; the top of the garden is Australia and South Africa – hot and dry – where proteas and banksias do well, and lower down it is shadier and so suits plants from New Zealand and Chile.

I found myself giddy, passing great banks of pelargoniums that are full-sized shrubs when I only grow them in a pot, and being towered over by huge palm trees and the silky foliage of *Leucadendron argenteum*, the silver tree – plants that I've previously seen only under glass. But then this is, as one visitor remarked, the Temperate House at Kew with the roof off.

Near the Abbey itself are massive rock faces dripping with succulents of all shapes and sizes, and winding paths through the West Rockery where, as well as succulents, the puyas, proteas and phormiums also push up from every fissure of the sun-baked rocks.

There are shady nooks where camellias thrive – though they bloom from November to January, rather than spring. There are masses of rhododendrons, bamboos and other exotics, and the range of plants is

constantly being added to. A new Mediterranean Garden is under construction – the first new area to be landscaped in 150 years. Tresco is not a stagnant garden – in keeping with the growth of its plants it is continuously moving on.

Before leaving I walk up to the monument erected in memory of Augustus Smith above New Grimsby. Below is the tower of Cromwell's Castle which sits, like a pepper pot, on a small headland jutting out into the channel, and reminds me that it is time to head for the boat.

I wind my way down the hill, seed lists and guidebooks under arm, and say goodbye on the quay at New Grimsby, from where *Sea King* takes her leave and heads for St Mary's. The sea is calmer still as the *Scillonian III* edges out of her berth at Hugh Town and heads for Penzance, and the sun is still high in the sky. My mind swims with pictures of palm trees and succulents, white sand and blue sea. The only sound, above the waves, is that of a helicopter flying overhead, packed full of passengers who booked in advance. They don't know what they missed.

Amid this confection of tropicality stands a gnarled old monkey-puzzle tree planted during the Victorian era.

BLENHEIM PALACE

Oxfordshire

KEEPING UP WITH the Joneses is one thing, but keeping up with the Marlboroughs is quite another. Even King George III said 'We have nothing to equal this.' Not one of his royal houses and palaces, thought Farmer George, could come close to matching the grandeur and splendour of Blenheim. If he had had the temperament of Henry VIII he would probably have turfed out the Duke of Marlborough and installed himself and his court. But he didn't, and the Palace and its extensive estate, given to John Churchill, the 1st Duke of Marlborough, by Queen Anne remains in the hands of the Spencer-Churchills.

It was the Royal Manor of Woodstock that was granted to the 1st Duke. So where did the name Blenheim come from? It came from the village of Blindheim in Bavaria, on the banks of the Danube, where Marlborough triumphed over the French at the Battle of Blenheim in 1704.

Not only did Queen Anne grant him the estate in her gratitude, but she also agreed to build him a house at her own

OPPOSITE The water terraces at Blenheim were designed by Achille Duchêne and built, under the beady eye of the 9th Duke of Marlborough, in the 1920s. They are on two levels and were dug out by hand – the spoil being removed on a custom-built railway.

expense. Munificent indeed! Especially as the architect commissioned to build the honey-stoned palace was Sir John Vanbrugh, already famous for designing Greenwich Hospital and Castle Howard in Yorkshire. Stone was shipped in from twenty quarries and the finest craftsmen were commissioned to work here. The Queen chipped in to the tune of £240,000, but then, wouldn't you just know it, funds were slow in coming and the Marlboroughs ended up providing around £60,000 themselves to see the initial

The Italian Garden, designed by Duchêne after the style of Le Nôtre, occupies a corner of the gardens between the East Wing and the Orangery, and comprises much intricately-clipped box and golden yew. A gilded mermaid fountain is in the centre and the orange trees stand out on the gravel in summer.

building through. While Marlborough himself was away winning battle after battle, Sarah, his Duchess, and the Queen were having battles of their own, and in 1710 they fell out for good.

Inside Vanbrugh's Grand Bridge are several rooms – some with fire-places and chimneys – though it is no longer considered safe to enter.

The Marlboroughs lived abroad from 1712 until the day after Queen Anne died in 1714, and then they returned to their stupendous palace to oversee its completion. Sir John Vanbrugh was dismissed in 1716 (the usual thing – economy versus quality) and the work was completed by James Moore and Nicholas Hawksmoor, who was Vanbrugh's adviser.

Vanbrugh and Hawksmoor – what an unbeatable combination! It was Hawksmoor who designed All Souls College in Oxford – two white pinnacles of perfection – as well as the west front of Westminster Abbey. Between them they

imbued Blenheim Palace with the most magical atmosphere.

But I'm racing ahead. We haven't arrived there yet. The village of Woodstock, on the A44 Evesham to Oxford road, has been spared much of the traffic that raced through it before the M40 was built. In summer it is still a busy Cotswold stone village, but Blenheim is worth visiting at any time of year. In winter nip into The Bear at Woodstock and toast your toes in front of its open fires before coming out of the front door and turning left along the handsome street. Past the church and a row of wonderful Georgian houses you'll find a left turn that takes you into Blenheim through Hawksmoor's Triumphal Arch. Narrow and lofty, this incredibly stately garden gate was commissioned by the

1st Duke's widow in 1723 – the year after his death. Pass through it, having paid the man in the uniform for your ticket, and you'll see what Randolph Churchill called 'The finest view in England'.

Below you on your right is 'Capability' Brown's magnificent lake, cut in half by Vanbrugh's elegant stone bridge. High upon the hill behind it is the pale grey Column of Victory, a forty-metre high memorial to the 1st Duke which was completed in 1730 at a cost of £3,000. It's a sort of rural Nelson's Column.

Around you are rolling acres of Brown's landscape and ahead of you the spreading wings of the yellow ochre palace topped with orbs of gold. Dawdle on this path to paradise. Whether you are on foot or in a car the lake seems to swim round behind you and the Palace hoves into view.

The weather never seems to matter. I have seen Blenheim in fair weather and foul, in mud and dust, in sun and sleet and still it is entrancing. There are sheep all around, grazing the close-cropped grass and bleating when disturbed. Geese and waterfowl glide across the lake and preen themselves on its banks; coots honk among the reeds. You can take a boat on the lake, or simply amble through hundreds of acres of park and woodland where coveys of pheasants run for cover at your approach. You can walk for miles and hardly see a soul. A visit to Blenheim provides you with boating, rambling and garden visiting all in the space of a day, and that without ever setting foot in the stately Palace.

The formal gardens at Blenheim were originally laid out by Vanbrugh and Queen Anne's head gardener Henry Wise, but 'Capability' Brown swept away the half-mile long Great Parterre on the south side to put in his great sweeps of grass and trees. What Brown created was a masterpiece, but you can understand why many think of him as a vandal.

Most of the formal gardens that surround the Palace today were commissioned

At the centre of the Italian Garden is the spectacularly-gilded Mermaid Fountain by the American sculptor Waldo Story.

in the 1920s by the 9th Duke, and designed by Achille Duchêne, a great admirer of Andre Le Nôtre, who designed the gardens at Versailles. The Italian Garden occupies a corner between the East Wing and the Orangery and is an intricate parterre of close-clipped box and golden yew. It fits the Palace like a glove. A gilded Mermaid Fountain forms the centre-piece and in summer orange trees stand on the gravel.

At the opposite end of the house are the water terraces, again designed by Duchêne, but with much input from the 9th Duke who would remind him: 'You are the Architect, I am the Duke.' No mistaking the pecking order there.

These water terraces really are something. Especially when you realise that they were dug out by hand using local labour and a custom-built railway rather like the kind you would find down a coal mine. They were originally planned on three levels but were eventually built on two, for fear that the lowest of the three would slide into the lake. These liquid parterres, elaborately constructed with clipped-box patterns between the pools, are centred with fountains shooting up into the air. Two rectangular pools occupy the lower level, which affords views across the lake to Brown's mature parkland.

The fountains are later additions, the 9th Duke having made it quite clear to Duchêne that 'Limpidity of water is pleasing and possesses a romance... Be careful not to destroy this major emotion which Nature has granted to you for the sake of what may possibly be a vulgar display of waterworks which can be seen at any exhibition or public park. Turn all these matters over in your mind.' Well, I rather like the fountains.

You can have a nice cup of tea and a bun on the topmost of the water terraces, and then walk down them to the bottom left-hand corner and take a turning that is signposted to the Rose Garden. The path winds between trees and then, on your left, with views across the lake to your right, stands a little summerhouse or, to give it its full title, the Temple of Diana. It was built for the 4th Duke by Sir William Chambers, the architect of the Pagoda in Kew Gardens, but its greater claim to fame is that within it, in the summer of 1908, a thirty-four-year-old Winston Churchill proposed to a twenty-three-year-old Clementine Hozier.

As Clementine sat on the bench she watched a beetle walking across the floor and said to herself: 'If that beetle reaches that crack and Winston has not proposed, then he is not going to.' He did, and they were married later that year.

Winston Churchill was born at Blenheim on 30 November 1874, the son of the Duke of Marlborough's second son, Randolph. Had the 8th Duke not had issue, Winston would have become Duke of Marlborough, although, said the 9th Duke, 'Much as he cared for Blenheim, it would not have appealed to him to go down in history as its owner, he had other and better ideas.'

That Churchill was fond of Blenheim there is no denying. He said: 'At Blenheim I took two very important decisions: to be born and to marry. I am happily content with the decisions I took on both these occasions.' He painted there, too, and there are samples of his work in the house.

Sir Winston Churchill died in 1965 and was given a state funeral the likes of which we children of the sixties had never seen before. But not for him an interment in Westminster Abbey. He was buried in Bladon churchyard on the edge of the estate. It's a simple and affecting village

When the water terraces were laid out, the 9th Duke of Marlborough wanted nothing to do with fountains, believing that they could possibly constitute a 'vulgar display of waterworks'. Fountains were added later and the effect is equally pleasing and in keeping with Blenheim's feeling of opulence and grandeur.

church with a squat tower. Around the back, as in many other village churchyards, are the grave-stones of local families – in this case the Marlboroughs. Look at the gravestones and piece together the family history. Winston and 'Clemmie' lie under a simple slab engraved with the words:

Winston Leonard Spencer Churchill
1874-1965
Clementine Ogilvy Spencer Churchill
1885-1977

The lower of the two water terraces has two pools and directly overlooks the lake. Within these pools are twin obelisks placed on rocky cairns that rise up out of the water, and around them are vast containers and columnar yews to emphasize the formality.

Churchill is remembered in a series of special rooms at Blenheim, near to the one in which he was born and you can walk round the gardens and grounds in his footsteps, musing on how they would have looked in the days when he was courting Miss Clementine Hozier.

On your right, after the Temple of Diana, you will come to the Rose Garden. It is not my favourite feature, sitting as it does in the middle of an arboretum where the magisterial trees are far more imposing. It is surrounded by a fence that must keep out rabbits – you can see evidence of them on the grass all around. Wander on down to the Grand Cascade, which was designed by 'Capability' Brown in the 1760s. If the weather has been dry, then you'll probably find yourself wondering what all the fuss is

about. But if the River Glyme is in spate then the tumbling of white foam over the tall embankment of boulders is as spectacular as a miniature Niagara. View it from the bridge in front, but watch your step in wet weather.

The most spectacular gardens are those that surround the Palace, but it is worth taking the narrow-gauge railway down to the Pleasure Gardens if you have children to entertain. Here they will find everything from a Butterfly House to a Bouncy Castle, a Herb Garden to a Model Village, and the Marlborough Maze, the largest symbolic hedge maze in the world. At just over an acre, the maze will be quite spectacular when fully mature, and there are twin platforms from which the Grinling Gibbons-inspired pattern can be viewed.

You will have guessed that this area is not my favourite. For me there is far more of the 'gosh' factor in the Grand Bridge and the Column of Victory than in an area that looks more like a garden centre. But you can't blame the Duke. Palaces and gardens like those at Blenheim cost a mint to maintain, and the Pleasure Gardens must go at least some way in helping to keep the wolf from the stately door. At least the narrow-gauge railway takes you to a spot that is well removed from the grandeur of two centuries ago before depositing you near the entrance of the Butterfly House.

When you do return to the Palace, look at the view across the lake and remind yourself that this stunning piece of natural-looking countryside is actually man-made. In 1705 the River Glyme was a trickle of a brook, margined by marshland and crossed by two small bridges. Originally Sir Christopher Wren was to have designed the new bridge, but Sir John Vanbrugh's grander scheme was eventually accepted.

Work began in 1708 and so much infill was needed to bring the bridge into contact with the banks at either side that earth had to be transported from the surrounding hills. For the bridge itself, Woodstock Manor was demolished and its masonry used in the river crossing.

Mind you, Vanbrugh and the Duchess all but came to blows over the extravagance of the structure. There are rooms inside it, some of them with fireplaces and chimneys. The Duchess complained that she had counted thirty-three rooms in it and that there was a house at each corner. Vanbrugh snapped back that if, when it was finished, she found a house there then she could go and live in it. There is no evidence that it was ever inhabited.

At this time the water continued to trickle under the great central arch in a canal. It was not until the 1760s that the River Glyme was dammed by 'Capability' Brown and two lakes created, one at either

Blenheim was designed by Sir John Vanbrugh, already famous for Castle Howard and Greenwich Hospital. He completed a building of immense grandeur which was subsequently surrounded by formal gardens and parkland that really do it justice.

side of the bridge. Then formality was swept away and the original intricately patterned gardens were submerged under a more natural landscape, just as the lower rooms of the bridge were submerged as Brown's lakes rose to complete the picture. I do find myself wondering if Brown ever had the slightest pricking of conscience when he banished all these formal gardens.

Cross the bridge from the Palace on foot (you can't take your car any further anyway) and turn to the left at the other side. Down by the lake you'll find an ancient spring, Rosamund's Well, said to have been known to Henry II's lover, the Fair Rosamund Clifford. Turn right over the bridge and you can walk round the upper lake, or Queen Pool, with its tree-bedecked island, past one of the many picturesque estate lodges and back to the Palace. One thing you will definitely discover is that ducks, geese and grass do not go together – wipe your shoes before you get back in the car!

Explore further afield among parkland and woodland before calling it a day, and when you leave, have a look at the stunning drystone wall that surrounds Woodstock Park. It is supposedly the first park wall to be built in England. Completed in its present form in 1729 it is between eight and nine miles long, eight feet high and two feet thick and cost an estimated £1,196 per mile.

Not all Blenheim is history. Today there are comprehensive tree-planting schemes overseen by the present 11th Duke to make sure that the estate stays in good heart. Lakes need to be dredged, fabric needs to be restored – but don't let all this worry you. Provide your support in the form of an entrance fee and then stay entranced for a day. It will take you at least that long to sample the delights of England's nearest equivalent to the Palace of Versailles.

CHELSEA FLOWER SHOW

London

THE THIRD WEEK in May is, for me, a kind of bookmark in my diary. It's a time of year when life comes to a standstill. No one expects to see me at home for at least five days, and work flies out of the window. The third week in May is 'Chelsea Week'.

Now you might argue that the Chelsea Flower Show isn't a garden at all, and you'd be right, it's about twenty-four gardens. They appear and disappear each year like 'Brigadoon' in the Lerner and Loewe musical. But for me, these gardens are as real as if they were there the whole year round, and they are the only ones in Britain you are certain to see at their absolute best. At Chelsea nobody is ever allowed to say: 'You should have been here last week.'

Along with these show-piece gardens comes the largest marquee in the world. It

covers three and a half acres and is filled to bursting with the best flowers, fruit and vegetables that gardeners can grow. I have never seen any point in arguing with the claim that this is the best flower show in the world, so perhaps you'll allow me the poetic licence of including it among my favourite gardens.

Since 1913, interrupted only by two world wars, the Royal Horticultural Society's Great Spring Show has sprung up in the grounds of the Royal Hospital, Chelsea – a wondrous example of Sir Christopher Wren's facility with a pencil, a ruler and some graph paper. Normally the handsome building, which is home to the scarlet-coated Chelsea Pensioners, looks down across lawns and tennis courts, and past a war memorial to the River Thames. I went by in a bus once and completely failed to recognise it without its frontage of canvas and awnings.

But, from midnight on the last Monday in April, the grounds in front of the Royal Hospital are leased to the Royal Horticultural Society for just forty days. In that time they must erect the Great Marquee and the trade stands down the avenues and provide catering and lavatory facilities.

The exhibitors must build their 'perfect gardens' in just three weeks and, at the end of the forty days, the grounds must be returned to the Royal Hospital. Broken kerbstones must be replaced and the grass revitalised. You'd hardly know that the Chelsea Flower Show had ever existed.

I first visited it in 1969 when I was a student at a horticultural college in Hertfordshire. After that I visited the show almost every year until, in 1983, I designed

The family garden I designed for Woman's Own *at the Chelsea Flower Show in 1983. A pink parasol sits on an octagonal terrace backed by white trellis, and the archway up which wisteria climbs doubles as a swing.*

OPPOSITE *A kitchen garden designed for* Country Living *by Rupert Golby has, as its centre-piece, a rustic gazebo with a stone roof. It looks as though it has been here for years – not just three weeks. Around it is a profusion of vegetables and a fountain made of bronze Brussels sprouts.*

and planted up a garden there for *Woman's Own* magazine. Since then 'Chelsea' has meant something quite special.

Some people think the show gardens at Chelsea are there all the time. They find it hard to believe that these 'ideal' landscapes are created in just three weeks on grass that is used as football pitches for the rest of the year. No, not by the pensioners, but by the local youth.

Preparation begins at least a year in advance, with applications being made to the Royal Horticultural Society and plans being submitted for approval. Nurserymen and growers will need to have worked their apprenticeship at some of the Society's Westminster shows before they are let loose at Chelsea. Designers of gardens need to convince the Society of their own quality of work and show that they are using

The students of Pershore College of Horticulture built this Lock Keeper's Garden for the Sunday Express. *The lock keeper's cottage and the narrow boat sit above the colourful garden, which has lush and varied streamside planting.*

contractors and plant suppliers who are up to scratch.

My plan was accepted, I had booked the lads – a ruddy-cheeked man, Mike Chewter, and his mate, Ray, who were Chelsea veterans – to build the 'hard landscape' part of the exhibit, and more plants than I knew what to do with had been ordered. We slogged away in some of the worst Chelsea weather that anyone had ever known. It rained for at least part of every day during the three weeks of preparation. We waded, we squelched and gradually the garden took shape – a family garden with a wooden-framed swing. I came in one morning to discover that someone had hung a noose on it.

The show grew nearer. Would we be ready in time?

We succeeded. It was a simple little family garden with a swing, a sand-pit and a millstone fountain, and it won us a Silver Gilt medal. Not a Gold. Still, it was our first time, and it had been a thrill to witness, at first hand, the Chelsea cama-raderie, the borrowing of this and that –

A 'Country Kitchen Garden' was the theme of my second garden at Chelsea. Herbs, vegetables, fruit and flowers were planted thickly to spill over the formal lines of this tiny plot. A white-painted beehive acted as a focal point against the woven willow wands of the fence.

'Have you any spare gravel? What have you got that I can fill that hole with?' – and the bacon sandwiches from the exhibitor's tent that kept us going. What's more, the rain stopped on the Monday morning and didn't start again until the bell rang to close the show at five o'clock on the Friday night. It sounds far fetched, but it's absolutely true.

Two years later *Woman's Own* decided they wanted to have another crack. I designed a 'Country Kitchen Garden', a simple plan for a forty-foot by twenty-foot garden with a brick path running direct to the front door, and two paths and a stream bisecting it at right angles to create eight square plots. The two patches nearest the gate had long grass speckled with cowslips and campions and dotted with dwarf apple trees. Water gushed out of an old cast-iron village pump and you crossed the stream over a plank bridge. There was a vegetable garden and a fruit patch, a gnarled old pear tree under which you could sit on iron-framed chairs, a herb garden, and two formal flower beds at either side of the front door. Two white-painted Chinese Chippendale benches from Chatsworth Carpenters sat in front

of the wattle hurdles that passed for a house front, and there was a beehive and a rhubarb forcing pot to add a flavour of the country.

Mike and Ray built a delectable knapped-flint wall into which the gate fitted, and the weather was kinder than it had been two years earlier. Plants arrived late and we worked like stink. Never in my life have I felt so tired.

I blush now to think what that garden cost. The final bill was around £12,000. Today some sponsors will spend up to £130,000. It's mind-blowing. And the tension builds as the judges prowl around. But I was pleased with my garden. It had been a slog, but there was such a tremendous sense of achievement and Mike and Ray were dead chuffed with their wall. It was a bit like being in the war together – we were all nervous and all completely drained.

But I had the *Chelsea Flower Show* television programme to take my mind off it. I slipped out of my muddied jeans and sweat shirt and into a rather natty striped blazer and bow-tie. In those early days Peter Seabrook and I would fill a fifty-five-minute programme on our own with, perhaps, a couple of guests and some music sequences. We would begin filming on Sunday afternoon and be on camera at six in the morning on Monday and Tuesday, with a lie in until eight on Wednesday. Most days ended at around seven in the evening and, on the Wednesday evening, we would sometimes be dubbing on the last bit of commentary at Television Centre fifteen minutes before transmission. 'Do you think you could pronounce the name correctly this time?' 'There's not much time left.' It doesn't half concentrate the mind.

Today, the timetable is much the same, though the inclusion of extra presenters does lighten the load, and the fact that modern cameras don't have to be cabled into the centre of the marquee from vast

wagons parked outside means that we can film after the public have been admitted.

Members' Days at Chelsea are Tuesday and Wednesday; the public are allowed in on Thursday and Friday, but the first official visitors have already had a look, even before the members get their turn.

Late on Monday afternoon the Royal Family pay their annual visit. The grounds are cleared of all those who should not be there and only one person is allowed to stand on each exhibit. At half past five on the evening of 20 May 1985 I stood by my Chelsea garden gate, having been released from filming, and savoured the stillness of the late afternoon. A coppery light bathed

Arabella Lennox-Boyd designed this garden for the Daily Telegraph. *The borders were planted up by John Metcalfe of Four Seasons Nursery who has a brilliant talent for form and colour – hot spots of red and purple catch the eye.*

the garden and, for the first time, I could relax and enjoy it. The beehive rose up above the blue-green cabbages and rhubarb peeped out of its forcing pot. Water gurgled from the village pump past the rushes and irises I had submerged in the stream and a blackbird came to bathe. The flints of Mike's and Ray's wall were bronze in the evening sun. The garden looked as though it had always been there.

My back ached and my hands felt like sandpaper, but I had at least managed to scrape most of the mud out from under my finger-nails. It was just as well. One by one the members of the monarchy were brought over to have a look. In my first year as an exhibitor they were whisked past. Well, I was a beginner and I hadn't really worked my passage. This year it was my turn. First Princess Alexandra, then Princess Michael of Kent, then the Princess Royal – all relaxed and laughing and interested. And then along came the towering figure of the President of the Royal Horticultural Society with the Queen. He carried a bowler hat in one hand and crooked a finger of the other in my direction. I went over to meet the Society's Patron.

The presentation, the introduction, and then I walked down the side of our garden – mine and Mike's and Ray's – and talked to the Queen about vegetables and irises and hollies for a good five minutes. She

Water features largely in gardens at Chelsea Flower Show, whether it is a spectacular water-fall or a modest pool with a fountain like this one designed for Yardley and the Daily Express *by an old hand at Chelsea, Geoffrey Whiten.*

'A Cottage Garden for Two' – the theme of the garden designed by Andrea Parsons for Help the Aged. The stonework is immaculate and the pergola links the two cottages across a terrace equipped with raised beds and a water feature.

smiled a lot. She said she preferred small vegetables to large ones, and she admired my irises. It was nice of her. The Princess Royal had, on the other hand, been rather scathing about the size of my gooseberries.

The royal party moved off to the tea tent, and the rest of us moved off for a well-earned drink of a rather stronger brew.

It's Tuesday morning, early. You walk to your garden to look for your card and see what kind of medal you have been awarded. I approached gingerly. At least the weather was good. A light dew; the plants would be refreshed. On a crisp spring morning the Thames Embankment is not such a bad place. The early morning sun was squinting through the towering plane trees behind my garden. I could see a white card on the brick path leading up to the front door. I found it hard to swallow, and then I saw the gold circle in the centre of the card. The Royal Horticultural Society's Gold Medal. I don't think I have ever felt so proud, or quite so emotional. Mike and Ray were convinced that their brickwork was the real secret of our success. The card hangs on my wall where, ten years on, it still gives me a thrill. And

so does the medal itself. They send it to you some months later, but only the first time you win it. After that you must make do with the card. I haven't built another Chelsea garden since then; it's good to quit while you are at the top. But I do hanker after it. Oh, yes; I do hanker.

What I have managed to do is present the *Chelsea Flower Show* programme for the BBC each year since that first one in 1983. It keeps me in touch with all those old friends I've known since I first came here in 1969, and it also allows me to enthuse about my passion for plants to a wider audience.

The gardens themselves – usually a couple of dozen – change every year. Some are rigidly formal, others are romantic and conjure up the paintings of Helen Allingham or Fragonard. Some are fantasy gardens – a scene from *The Wind in the Willows* or a bit of the seaside – others are smart but practical. What they all have in common is their standard of perfection.

Now there are those who have become blasé, or even cynical, about Chelsea. Some say it is too commercial and that it was never intended to be so. Well, I can't go along with that. Chelsea has always been a place where professional British gardeners demonstrate their skills. They bring along plants which have been grown for a year or more especially for this show of shows, and they spend a week dispensing free advice to anyone who asks for it. They're not even allowed to sell plants at the show, they may only take orders. It's undoubtedly a commercial exercise, but one which has hardly become commercialised in the pejorative sense of the word.

The sundriesmen are allowed to sell from their stalls, but only those items under four feet in length. Well it's difficult to manoeuvre a six-foot-long hoe through a packed showground!

Mind you, on the Friday at the end of the week, many of the plants are sold off once the bell has rung at five o'clock. It's then that you see folk of all ages lugging plants of all shapes and sizes across the Chelsea and Albert bridges. Sloane Square tube station turns into a floral fiesta as the determined owners of seven-foot-tall delphiniums try to get them through the doors of a tube train without snapping them off.

But my favourite moment at the Chelsea Flower Show happens earlier in the week. On Monday evening there is a Royal Charity Gala when, for a three-figure sum, you can look at the show in the select company of the royal family and others who have splashed out on a ticket. Champagne flows freely, there are canapés on silver trays, and boot blackers to clean your dusty shoes for a donation to charity. It's a great occasion, but it's the Tuesday morning that I savour most.

My press pass allows me into the show-ground at half past five in the morning. All the exhibitors who have toiled through the night have gone home; they'll not be back for at least an hour. I leave my bag in the television crew's caravan and walk towards the Great Marquee. I unpick the rope that holds down a canvas flap and slip into a floral paradise.

Completely alone I wander between banks of roses and sweet peas, delphiniums and begonias, past miniature alpine land-scapes and displays of exotic blooms from South Africa, Barbados, Australia and the Eastern Caribbean. The air is fresh and fragrant and around me are the most perfect flowers all timed to be at their best right now. The growers of all these floral riches are about to heave their weary bones out of bed and come to discover which medal they have won. But I shall know before they do. I wander softly among this incredible Eden that has, at five-thirty on Tuesday morning, been put together just for me, and every year, without fail, there comes a moment when I can no longer see for the tears.

The Rock Bank at Chelsea is the place for traditional rock gardens such as this one which was designed and built by Peter Tinsley. It is planted up with alpines, rhododendrons and dwarf conifers. A stream tumbles down over granite boulders to a pool below.

GARDENS INFORMATION

Please note that some of these gardens are privately owned and will only be opened on a limited number of days. It is advisable to telephone all gardens for confirmation of opening hours prior to visiting.

BETH CHATTO GARDENS
Elmstead Market, Essex
TELEPHONE (01206) 822007
Open daily except
Sunday and Bank Holidays

BIDDULPH GRANGE
Grange Road, Biddulph, Staffordshire
TELEPHONE (01782) 517999
Open Wednesday to Sunday
and Bank Holiday Mondays

BLENHEIM PALACE
Woodstock, Oxfordshire
TELEPHONE (01993) 811325
Palace and Gardens open daily
mid March to end October
Park open daily throughout the year

CASTLE HOWARD
York, North Yorkshire
TELEPHONE (01653) 648444
Grounds and House open daily
mid March to late October

CASTLE OF MEY
Caithness, Highlands
TELEPHONE (0195 586) 209
Open to the public
under the auspices of
Scotland's Garden Scheme
on two days in July and one day in September

CHATSWORTH
Bakewell, Derbyshire
TELEPHONE (01246) 582204
Open daily
Easter to end October

CHELSEA FLOWER SHOW
Royal Hospital, Chelsea, London
TELEPHONE (0171) 828 1744
Open Tuesday to Friday during third week in May

CRATHES CASTLE
Crathes, by Banchory, Grampian
TELEPHONE (01330) 844525
Open daily
beginning April to end October

GREAT DIXTER
Northiam, East Sussex
TELEPHONE (01797) 252878
Open daily except Monday

HAMPTON COURT PALACE
East Molesey, Surrey
TELEPHONE (0181) 781 9500
Open daily except
24, 25 and 26 December

HATFIELD HOUSE
Hatfield, Hertfordshire
TELEPHONE (01707) 262823
House open Tuesday to Sunday
East Gardens open Monday afternoons
West Gardens open daily 25 March to
second Sunday in October

HELMINGHAM HALL
Stowmarket, Suffolk
TELEPHONE (01473) 890363
Open Sunday
end April to early September
Open Wednesday by appointment

HIDCOTE MANOR
Chipping Campden, Gloucestershire
TELEPHONE (01386) 438333
Open daily except Tuesday and Friday
beginning April or Easter
(whichever is the earlier)
to end October

HINTON AMPNER
Hinton Ampner, Alresford, Hampshire
TELEPHONE (01962) 771305
House and Garden open Tuesday and Wednesday
Garden only Saturday and Sunday
(afternoons only)
beginning April to end September

HODNET HALL
Hodnet, Market Drayton, Shropshire
TELEPHONE (01630) 685202
Open Tuesday to Sunday and Bank Holiday Mondays
beginning April to end September

HOLKER HALL
Cark-in-Cartmel, Cumbria
TELEPHONE (015395) 58328
Open daily except Saturday
beginning April to end October

INVEREWE
Poolewe, Wester Ross
TELEPHONE (01445) 781200
Open daily throughout the year

LANHYDROCK
Bodmin, Cornwall
TELEPHONE (01208) 73320
House open Tuesday to Sunday
and Bank Holiday Mondays
beginning April or Easter
(whichever is the earlier)
to end October
Garden open daily throughout the year

1 LISTER ROAD
London
TELEPHONE (0181) 556 8962
Open to the public under the auspices of the National
Gardens Scheme on one Sunday in August
Private visits by arrangement

PACKWOOD HOUSE
Lapworth, Warwickshire
TELEPHONE (01564) 782024
Open Wednesday to Sunday
beginning April to end October

PARCEVALL HALL GARDENS
Appletreewick, North Yorkshire
TELEPHONE (01756) 720311
Open daily
Good Friday to end October
Winter by arrangement

POWIS CASTLE
Welshpool, Powys
TELEPHONE (01938) 554336
Open Wednesday to Sunday
beginning April or Easter
(whichever is the earlier)
to end October
Also open Tuesday and Bank Holiday Mondays
during July and August.

ROYAL BOTANIC GARDENS
Kew, Richmond, Surrey
TELEPHONE (0181) 940 1171
Open daily except
25 December and 1 January

SISSINGHURST CASTLE GARDEN
Cranbrook, Kent
TELEPHONE (01580) 712850
Open daily except Monday
(including Bank Holiday Mondays)
2 April to 15 October
Woodland and Lake Walks
open daily throughout the year

SNOWSHILL MANOR
Snowshill, Near Broadway, Worcestershire
TELEPHONE (01386) 852410
Open daily except Tuesday and Good Friday
beginning April to end October

STICKY WICKET
Buckland Newton, Dorchester, Dorset
TELEPHONE (01300) 345476
Open Thursday only
mid June to mid September

STUDLEY ROYAL
*Fountains Abbey and Studley Royal, Studley Park,
Ripon, North Yorkshire*
TELEPHONE (01765) 608888
Abbey and Garden open daily
except 24 and 25 December
and Friday in November, December and January

TATTON PARK
Knutsford, Cheshire
TELEPHONE (01565) 750780
Gardens open Tuesday to Sunday throughout the year
Park open daily except Monday
23 October to 31 March

TREBAH
Mawnan Smith, Falmouth, Cornwall
TELEPHONE (01326) 250448
Open daily throughout the year

TRESCO ABBEY
Tresco, Isles of Scilly, Cornwall
TELEPHONE (01720) 422868
Open daily throughout the year

WOODROYD
Hampshire
Not open to the public

INDEX

Entries in italics refer to photographs